The American Drive-In Movie Theater

Don Sanders and Susan Sanders

MOTORBOOKS
INTERNATIONAL

DEDICATION

This book is dedicated to our daughters, Calvert and Genevieve, and to those who are too young to have experienced this great chapter in American history.

This edition published in 2003 by Motorbooks International, an imprint of MBI Publishing Company, Galtier Plaza, Suite 200, 380 Jackson Street, St. Paul, MN 55101-3885 U.S.A.

© Don Sanders and Susan Sanders, 1997, 2003

First published in 1997 as *The American Drive-In Movie Theatre* by MBI Publishing Company.

The information in this book is true and complete to the best of our knowledge. All recommendations are made without any guarantee on the part of the author or Publisher, who also disclaim any liability incurred in connection with the use of this data or specific details.

We recognize that some words, model names and designations, for example, mentioned herein are the property of the trademark holder. We use them for identification purposes only. This is not an official publication.

Motorbooks International titles are also available at discounts in bulk quantity for industrial or sales-promotional use. For details write to Special Sales Manager at Motorbooks International Wholesalers & Distributors, Galtier Plaza, Suite 200, 380 Jackson Street, St. Paul, MN 55101-3885 U.S.A.

ISBN 0-7603-1707-0

On the front cover: The drive-in movie theater saw its most prosperous years during the late 1950s. This illustration of a typical ozoner in 1959 presents all the wonderful elements of the drive-in experience. Close friends, great cars, good food, and a science fiction flick all contributed to a perfect night out. *Jon Letness, Graphics 400*

On the frontispiece: The most popular name for a drive-in movie theater was "Starlite." The Starlite Drive-In in Birmingham, Alabama, featured a marquee illuminated with glorious neon lights. *Wagner Zip-Change, Inc.*

On the title page: Drive-in movie theaters made excellent subjects for postcards. This postcard for a drive-in theater in Phoenix, Arizona, advertised that patrons could watch "movies under the stars." *From the authors' collection.*

On the back cover, top: The Circle Drive-In circa 1964. During the heyday of the drive-in, many owners hired artists and neon glass workers to design the otherwise empty side of the screen tower. When the Circle was originally built in 1947, the theater sported a Native American-themed mural. When the painting became worn, it was replaced with a bear, the mascot of the local college, Baylor University. *Windy Drum 1964, from the James Jasek collection.* **Middle left:** The Everett Motor Movie Theater in Everett, Washington, used the Native-American design motif employed by many drive-ins and other roadside attractions of the day. *Planet of the Apes* and *One Million Years B.C.* were typical of the campy sci-fi adventure movies that gained an audience in the late 1960s with the help of drive-in movie theaters. *From the authors' collection.* **Middle right:** One dollar for a drive-in movie experience seems like a steal by today's standards. Look closely at these tickets and you'll see that, before tax, the admission price was actually only 83 cents, and that's per car! *From the authors' collection.* **Bottom:** Various Filmack trailers motivated moviegoers to buy food before or between shows. Hot dogs were always a staple of any concession stand and are still served in many theaters. *Filmack/Mark Bialek.*

Printed in Hong Kong

CONTENTS

ACKNOWLEDGMENTS

There are not enough words of praise and gratitude for our dear friend Jon Bokenkamp. His wonderful knowledge of film, his lively and engaging writing style, and his devotion to the drive-in movie theater all made him the perfect person to bring our thoughts and words to life. After spending countless hours listening to us talk about the material for this book, he combined our thoughts with his knowledge to create it. We thank him for making that part of the journey such a pleasant one.

We also want to thank the following people for their extraordinary contributions to this project: Andy Reisberg for being the first person to ignite Don's interest and for saving beautiful drive-in photographs; A. J. Roquevert for loving movie theaters enough to collect important memorabilia and for patiently and generously sharing so much of it with us; Ralph Bieber, Raymond Harris, and Pacific Theatres for trusting us with their priceless original photographs; Annette Funicello for so graciously granting an interview; and Mark Bialek for dedicating his time, energy, and resources to the preservation of the drive-in movie theater.

We are very grateful to hundreds of individuals and organizations for providing us with support, materials, and friendship during the past 10 years. The following list, which is in no particular order, attempts to thank many of them:

Don Risley, Steve Fitch, Kim Bialek, Rob Innis, John Murphy, Brian Johnson, Vincent Mizzi, Rob Giles, Andy Hanson, Mary Koon, Tanja Lindstrom, John Bloom, Tim Buck, Sue Hargroder, Jack Corgan, Jack Corgan, Jr., Corgan Architects, Suzanne McKee, Brent Byers, James Tucker, Elizabeth Reid Murray, Sue Bright Richter, Bradford S. Tucker, Charles Von Rosenberg, Frankie Avalon, The Honorable Kay Bailey Hutchison, Governor Ann Richards, Steven E. Massengill, Cindy Deppe, Jim Goble, Evil Sam Graham, Tim Thompson, Tim Reed, Wanger Zip-Change, Inc., Curt Teich Postcard Archives, Bobby Butler, Donald C. Brown, Jr., Rosemary and Jim Costello, Daniel Collins, Dallas Historical Society, John Pronk, Kevin Calvert, Paul Taylor, *Route 66* magazine, David Burd, Peter Ness, Phyllis Collazo, Kirk Dooley, Andrew Shane, Doug Hailey, Brian and Jerry Poblocki, N.A.T.O., Mary Ann Grasso, Liz and Larry Bleiberg, Larry Powell, Tony Click, Jack Coleman, Curtis Meadows, Lawrence and Debrean Loy, Brian Butko, Tom Spelts, Norton Stein, Bob Ray Sanders, Dollie Gentry, David Woodworth, Chan Wood, Robert Mack, Filmack Studios, Lillian Rae and Rex A. Sanders, Bertha and Leslie Riley, Wilson Goss, Dorothy Sain, Trinity Lutheran Church of Stillwater, Minnesota, Nancy Moore, Keith Murphy, Janiece and Rich Peterson, Jack Savage, Larry Rodkey, Bill Sohl, Barbara Weiher, George Rosser, Dwayne Jones, Jim Heimann, Wesley Horton, Vivian Breshears, Leni Howe, Kyle Klassen, Skip Yassenhoff, Dr. Robert H. Schuller, Claudia Holloway, Crystal Cathedral Ministries, Kay Valentine, Terrence Wharton, Bill Munster, Alexander Troup, Ron Chan, Warner Brothers, Inc., Lorraine Santoli, Don Lott, Pete Phillips, *Movie Maker* magazine, Stephen J. Coan, Ford Motor Company, Sandra Nichols, Russell Koontz, Society for Commercial Archaeology, Eric Price, Richard Jackson, Brigham Young University, Lana Guiler, Arlene Hogue, Louis Rukeyser, Kipp Teague, Ruth Lloyd, Bruce Shinabarger, Sam Kirkland, O. Winston Link, Thomas Garver, University of South Alabama Archives, Paul Geissinger, Institute of Texas Cultures, Michael Karl Witzel, Temple Hall, Academy of Motion Picture Arts and Sciences, George Toomer, Cleveland Public Library, James Jasek, Dallas Public Library, Hawaii State Archives, Bishop Museum, Reverend Louis H. Yim, University of Texas Arlington Library, *LaMesa Press Reporter*, Russell Skiles, Henry Ford Museum, The Walt Disney Company, Larson Campbell, Heather Melzig, Nicole Seanor, Alison Whittington, Ralph Lomma, Druce Riley, Ange Kedersha, Leslie Swiggart, Gary Haley, Linda Mitchell Adams, Kim Walter, Great Eastern Theatres, Jim Lupima, Will Anderson, Robert Fossum, *Roadside* magazine, Eddie Lou Ayres, *Texas Highways* magazine, Michael A. Murphy, Graceland, Jeanne Johnson Phillips, Beaches Historical Society, Debbi Mikash, Pikes Peak Library District, Camden County Historical Society, Morgan Entrekin, Jean E. Felton, Kay McCarthy, Theatre Historical Society of America, Historical Society of Western Pennsylvania, Del Norte County Historical Society, Casey Krasula, Octavio Olvera, Bill Hannah, *Fort Worth Star-Telegram,* University of California-Santa Cruz, Grand Rapids Public Library, The *Andy Griffith* Rerun Watchers Club, *Bewitched* and Elizabeth Montgomery Site, *Munsters* Web Ring, Stefanie Wittenbach, Southwest Collection at Texas Tech University, Shirley Aplay, The Honorable J. C. Watts, William L. Perry, Gannett News Service, Margaret A. McGurk, *The Cincinnati Inquirer*, Dennis de la Paz, Dwight Wilson, Jim Crotty, Jim Wheat, Tony Ventura, Scott Drane, and David Lounder.

Finally, we will always be indebted to Motorbooks International for having the desire to publish a book on the subject of drive-in movie theaters and for giving us the opportunity to be their partner. We appreciate their faith in us.

—Don and Susan Sanders

PREFACE

My father traveled extensively when I was a child. He was a Texas salesman, and after World War II, it seemed that he was always on the road. Many times I would join him on the highway, eagerly awaiting the next stop for roadside sandwiches, sodas, and French fries. New Mexico, Arizona, Colorado—the road took us everywhere.

As I got older, my parents and I began to take a yearly summer vacation. It was the two weeks I looked forward to all year long. We'd pack the Oldsmobile and embrace the road. It was two weeks of nothing but picnics, souvenir stands, and national parks. It seemed like we traveled everywhere those early years—Pike's Peak, Disneyland, The Petrified Forest, New York City, Mount Rushmore, the Grand Canyon, and Washington D.C. You name it, the Sanders family was there! It was from my father that I gained this great appreciation for travel—trips that couldn't have been possible without road maps, tire irons, and air-conditioners that hook onto the window. It wasn't the type of travel where everyone hops in a jetliner with their cell phone and goes off to a phony resort for a week. The car and the road took us to deserts, mountains, and plains. That was my childhood.

But when I met my wife, Susan, I realized that not everyone had been blessed with my innate sense of the road. Susan's father loved to read and, as noble and important as reading is, it's simply not as adventuresome or romantic. Rather, Susan's world of travel consisted of three trips a week to ballet school. And although she's an incredible dancer to this day, her family simply did not have the money to take these great little journeys.

When Susan and I started dating in 1989, travel became an important part of our relationship. We would take road trips for dates. Sometimes we would travel to Oklahoma or Arkansas, but wherever we went, we had a great time. It was a way for Susan to actually see the roadside America that she missed as a child, and it was a way for me to relive some of the best memories of my young life.

Over the years, our travels continued to grow, and we started to become more interested in the old buildings and businesses along the highway. Of particular interest was the drive-in theater. At first, I would snap a picture or two of an old drive-in as we would pass it by. But we soon found ourselves on a quest to see how many drive-in theaters we could find. Where were they? Were they still operating? There is no documentation of such theaters, and so Susan and I took it upon ourselves to find out. Susan fell in love with the individual architecture of each structure while I found myself becoming increasingly involved in taking pictures and digging up old drive-in theater photography. As the trips and years went by, I began to accumulate a huge collection of drive-in theater photographs. I would hang them on the walls, or keep them in folders, but I never really had a way to show them to others. It was Susan who ultimately suggested that we put them together into a book. And so this project was born.

When we talk to people about drive-in theaters, they immediately turn on to the subject matter. After all, who doesn't remember going to the drive-in as a kid? I used to frequent the Belknap, the Century 4, and the Fort Worth Twin in my youth. Susan vividly remembers going to the Tem-Bel Drive-In on a date with a boyfriend who wanted to do everything *but* watch the movie. Everyone has a memory.

It is our hope that this book stands as a monument to the drive-in theater. In our minds, the drive-in theater of the late-1940s and early-1950s was the greatest entertainment there ever was or will be. Where else could you go and see a movie, see the stars, have dinner cooked for you, ride a pony, have your laundry done, show off your new Chevy, or ride in the trunk and feel like you accomplished something by sneaking in? The drive-in theater was a high point in American popular culture.

CHAPTER 1

PREVIEW OF COMING ATTRACTIONS 1900 to 1945

The American automobile and the motion picture were born just 12 years apart. The automobile—a Duryea—started chugging down the street in 1893, and the motion picture came to life in 1905. Since that time they have shaped the way our nation lives. The hybridization of these two novelties brought about a tremendous change in this country. After all, who could picture an America without highways or drive-throughs, without motion pictures or Hollywood, or without the drive-in theater?

America was virtually built around the automobile. It transformed our lives by allowing the everyday family to determine where and when it would travel. We could take a family vacation to the Grand Tetons—everything for survival packed neatly into the back of the car—or roadtrip to grandma's house for a Thanksgiving feast. Whatever we did, wherever we went, we were free! Distance no longer mattered. One of the most important inventions of the 20th century was at our fingertips.

But it wasn't enough.

History shows that people were itching to watch outdoor movies before the technology of motion pictures had even been completely developed. Ironically, it was at the turn of the century in Hawaii (which had not yet become a U.S. territory) that large communities would gather and watch silent Kinescope films projected on the outsides of local buildings. According to Reverend Louis H. Yim, a church historian with the Saint Pius X Church, the open air theater was located on a vacant lot in the city of Honolulu. In fact, the church's Sacred Hearts Convent School, which was founded in 1859, can be seen in the background. The audience for this particular show in 1906 was made up of native Hawaiians and Haole (non-native Caucasian residents of Hawaii). Obviously, the tradition of entertaining under the stars was developing early. Hawaii State Archives

Mr. Charles Von Rosenberg, right, of Halletsville, Texas, recalls frequenting indoor theaters during the 1920s with no roof, just four walls. These movie houses were known as airdromes, and were much like a fenced-off field. Wooden benches provided seating for about 150 people, while the local piano teacher would tickle the ivories to accompany the film. Such theaters, which were common in many parts of the country, were often equipped with small heaters so patrons could watch silent movies under the stars without getting too cool. But the heat rose and the rain fell. And although the airdrome never caught on, it was one step in the transition from indoor to outdoor theaters. Charles Von Rosenberg

Just as the automobile was being set before the American consciousness, the motion picture began to infiltrate the entertainment industry. And just as fascinating as the automobile was the mechanical novelty of moving film. Vaudeville had long been a primary means of entertainment, but the nickelodeon theaters were about to explode across the country. For only 5 cents one could watch a moving picture. By the middle of the second decade, the technology of the "silent cinema" had swallowed vaudeville. Silent pictures swept the nation as Charlie Chaplin and Buster Keaton danced on screen. They made us laugh and we were willing to pay them to do so.

By the end of World War I, the United States hungered for even more entertainment and recreational activities. America's society and attitude changed, and at the center of this transformation were the car and movie. "The motion picture and the automobile came about during a time of great social revolution in this country," explains film historian and preservationist David Shepard. "America was changing from an artisan econ-

omy, where everyone took care of their own needs, to an economy where leisure became a commodity that could be marketed like breakfast cereal." The automobile and the motion picture happened to be a natural way to fulfill this desire for leisure. The two entities spawned a type of natural phenomenon.

Influencing and propelling the postwar American leisure culture were the returning soldiers and sailors. Their impact was felt everywhere, including the motion picture industry. During the World War, it was common for Hollywood to donate prints of movies to the Armed Forces as part of its contribution to the wartime effort. These films, often shown outdoors, allowed personnel to unwind and relax. After the war, veterans of the Armed Forces, who were accustomed to watching films in a less formal element than provided by traditional movie palaces, wanted to "interact" with the films. They liked to whoop and drink and cut loose, a type of behavior that was not allowed at conventional indoor theaters. Teenagers, who were not in the war, were influenced and reacted in a similar manner. Young Americans were getting restless and a natural transposition was beginning to take place.

Car culture was starting to get established, and teens began to tinker with the notion of independence. After all, there was no privacy at home—mom and pop were ever-present. For this reason, an enclosed automobile became an excellent place for inti-

The practice of watching movies under the stars continued to take shape. Much like the theaters Charles Von Rosenberg remembers from his childhood is this 1915 Air Dome Theater, which stood on Fremont Street in Las Vegas, Nevada. University of Nevada Las Vegas

11

Travelers among early Grace Lines passenger ships could enjoy a movie under the stars informally. Standard projection equipment was used while a 15 x 15-foot screen was strapped between two poles, which also supported the outdoor speaker system. Many of the passengers watched the film from the swimming pool deck while up to 52 additional passengers viewed the screen from either the verandah cafe or the sundeck with equal ease. Both passengers and crew members could watch the programs, which consisted of one feature and one short.

California, which is known for its fascination with car culture, received its first drive-in, The Pico Drive-In, on September 9, 1934.

macy. Windows steamed and back seat romance flourished! Yet there was still one problem—"parking" was illegal. In many rural towns across the nation, local law officials made sure that teens didn't take their love to the country roads. And it was strictly enforced. So, where could an eager couple take an automobile and park? Where could they be alone?

The drive-in theater as we know it would not be realized until America's two greatest icons were married. Who could have guessed that it would take a salesman from New Jersey to make the introduction?

The Drive-In Theater Is Born

The year was 1933, and Richard M. Hollingshead felt that Americans were ready for a change. A businessman by trade, Hollingshead was owner of Whiz Auto Products Company, a business founded by his father in which he pedaled various oils, soaps, and greases for automobile care. Trying to find a niche market, Hollingshead "analyzed the market from the standpoint of what people gave up last. It

Richard M. Hollingshead, Jr.— The "Father of the Drive-In Theater"

Opening night at Hollingshead's Camden Drive-In Theatre was quite a success. In the center, a willing usher awaits to escort patrons who stray from the well-lighted path. Camden County Historical Society

As the story goes, it all happened in the driveway of Hollingshead's Riverton, New Jersey, home. Trying to find a way to combine America's two great love affairs—the automobile and the movies—Hollingshead sat a Kodak 16mm projector on the hood of his car and spooled up some old home movies. He parked the car so he could face a screen he had strategically hung in a nearby tree. Behind the screen, Hollingshead placed his radio to face the car. He sat in the car that night and watched the movies. With the windows up or down, he could still hear the radio. He then tried to simulate rain by carefully placing his lawn sprinkler above the car; the image was still decent. The next step was to devise a way in which individuals could see over the car parked ahead of them. After weeks of parking cars in various arrangements, Hollingshead developed a ramp system in which the front of each car was pointed upwards, angled toward the screen. This would later become the basis of his patent. "Inveterate smokers rarely enjoy a movie because of the smoking prohibition," said Hollingshead to a local paper shortly before his brainchild opened to the public in the summer of 1933. "In the Drive-In theater, one may smoke without offending others. People may chat or even partake of refreshments brought in their cars without disturbing those who prefer silence. The Drive-In theater idea virtually transforms an ordinary motor car into a private theater box. The younger children are not permitted in the movie theaters and are frequently discouraged even when accompanied by parents or guardians. Here the whole family is welcome, regardless of how noisy the children are apt to be and parents are furthermore assured of the children's safety because youngsters remain in the car. The aged and infirm will find the Drive-In a boon because they will not be subjected to inconvenience such as getting up to let others pass in narrow aisles or the uncertainty of a seat."

Evidently, the townspeople agreed with Hollingshead's ideas. That theater opened to a full house on June 6, 1933.

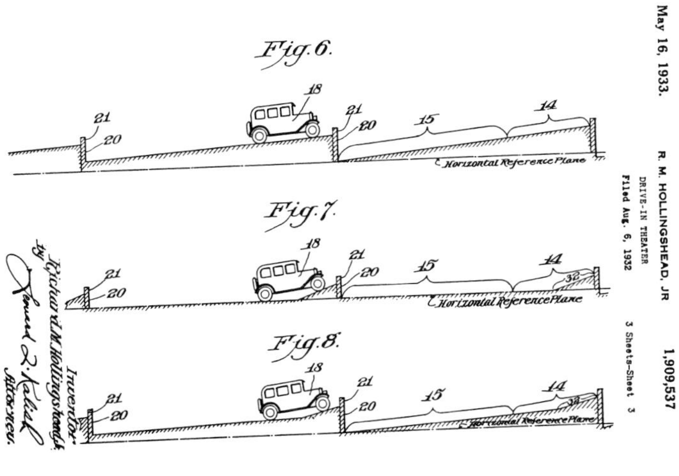

Just 10 months after filing his patent, Hollingshead had the Camden Drive-In Theatre open for business. This drawing from his original patent shows three different views of how cars would be pointed at the screen. Camden County Historical Society

Fig. 6.

Fig. 7.

Fig. 8.

May 16, 1933.

R. M. HOLLINGSHEAD, JR
DRIVE-IN THEATER
Filed Aug. 6, 1932

1,909,537

3 Sheets-Sheet 3

This 1940 photograph shows the world's oldest operating drive-in, Shankweiler's Drive-In Theatre. As you can see, the setting is somewhat rural. In the foreground is Mr. Shankweiler's hotel and in the background a ballpark. At one time, the theater even boasted of a landing strip for airplanes. The new screen tower, which is shown in this photograph, replaced the first screen, which simply consisted of two telephone poles and a white sheet. Paul Geissinger

Eager patrons line up to see a movie at The Pico Drive-In in Los Angeles. As seen in this 1934 photograph, the theater owners neglected to pour a permanent concrete driveway. Rather, stones were placed to keep cars neatly in line. University of Southern California Library

came out this way: Food. Clothing. Autos. Movies. In that order." His original idea was to create a Hawaiian-village-theme gas station complete with thatched roofs, gas pumps resembling palm trees, and an automobile service area. The station would also provide outdoor movies during the otherwise poor nighttime business hours. This concept was intended to give the station a gas sales edge throughout the evening while providing an outlet to sell more Whiz Auto Products items. Oddly enough, the service station idea was dropped, but Hollingshead continued to tinker with the notion of an outdoor theater.

Hollingshead considered the problems of the movie houses at the time: "The mother says she's not dressed; the husband doesn't want to put on his shoes, the question is what to do with the kids; then how to find a baby sitter; parking the car is difficult or maybe they have to pay for parking; even the seats in the theater may not be comfortable

An early advertisement for the Pico Drive-In does not list the name of the theater, as there were no other theaters to mistake it for. The name "Pico," which was the nearest street, wasn't added until some time after the theater opened. Jim Heimann

While the early days were a slow start, many people with no previous experience in theatrical presentation began to build their own drive-in theaters. Here, a projection booth is under construction in the early 1930s. Department of Special Collections, University of California Los Angeles

The framework of massive screen towers, such as the one shown here, were constructed on the ground. Department of Special Collections, University of California Los Angeles

To eliminate sound complaints from nearby (and in some cases not-so-nearby) neighbors, drive-ins employed various new technologies. This system at the Sun-Val Drive-In of Burbank, California, attempted a crude version of the in-car speaker. Here, each car pulled up in front of its own speaker, which would then blast the sound back at the car. While the entire sound system was operated by only one volume control, each row of speakers could be turned off or on by the projectionist. The benefit of such a system was that empty rows could be turned off, thus eliminating excess noise pollution on slow nights. If a train or truck passed near the theater, the ticket girl would signal the projectionist to turn up the volume. Pacific Theatres

 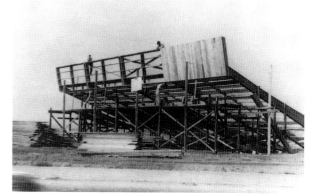

The Saco Drive-In in Saco, Maine, was billed as "The Showplace of Maine." Located along U.S. Route 1, the pioneer drive-in was built in 1939 by Eugene V. Boragine and offered a variety of amenities. It featured a kiddie park, dance floor, and large terrace for added enjoyment. Brian Butko

An early story and accompanying advertisement for the world's first drive-in movie theater, which opened in Camden, New Jersey, June 6, 1933. Also shown is a later advertisement for that same drive-in theater. Paul Geissinger

to contemplate." Hollingshead recognized that while movie lovers may not have been happy with the theatrical logistics of the day, everyone seemed to truly enjoy the comfort of their automobile.

With this in mind, Hollingshead experimented with various parking arrangements and theater layouts that would make it possible to view a movie from one's car. He tampered with screen sizes and various projector throw lengths, and he devised a crude sound system. Now, that first sound system was a doozy. It wasn't the small box-like speakers we know today; that technology would not come until much later. Rather, Hollingshead adapted an RCA system that used three central speakers to blast sound from behind the screen. RCA referred to this technology "as controlled directional sound." Unfortunately,

there was no individual volume control. This meant that everyone in the drive-in theater heard the same level of sound. Even worse, the cars in the back rows heard the sound later than those in the front rows. Years later, Hollingshead joked that, "if the wind was right, you could hear that soundtrack in homes a couple miles away." He quickly developed a ramping design that would allow one customer to see over the top of another. With the concept solidified, he submitted an application to the United States Patent Office on August 6, 1932.

Hollingshead soon partnered up with his first cousin Willie Warren Smith of Riverton, New Jersey, and founded Park-In Theaters. After securing additional capital from other minor backers, Hollingshead was able to break ground. On May 14, 1933, the same

day his patent was granted, construction began on the world's first drive-in theater. Within just three short weeks, he was ready for business.

On June 6, 1933, The Automobile Movie Theater opened for business. Ads ran in the local paper, and the owners pounded the pavement all day inviting the people of Camden out for an evening of entertainment under the stars. The cost was a single quarter. That first feature was *Wife Beware*, starring Adolphe Menjou. By the time the drive-in opened, *Wife Beware* was well into its second-run status, but because distributors did not want to compete with the local indoor theater, they were not willing to book a more enticing release. Three shows ran nightly; 8:30, 10, and 11 PM. Later, however, one screening was eliminated and the schedule revised with shows at 8:45 and 10:45.

Imitations quickly began to pop up. On April 15, 1934, Shankweiler's Auto Park

New York's first open-air drive-in theater was the Valley Stream Drive-In located on Long Island, New York. This photograph, taken in August of 1938, shows the theater's giant screen and marquee, which urges motorists to come "sit in your car." The 12-acre lot accommodated 500 automobiles. UPI/Bettmann

Owners of the Valley Stream Drive-In stand behind the theater's huge neon sign. Notice that a new show was brought to the theater three times a week and that two shows would be played nightly regardless of the weather conditions. UPI/Bettmann

A young uniformed attendant directs a father and son through the field to place the car on one of the ramps at the Valley Stream Drive-In. UPI/Bettmann

opened in Orefield, Pennsylvania. Even more primitive than the theater in Camden, Shankweiler's was equipped with only one overhead speaker that provided sound to the entire audience. In addition to offering the people of the Lehigh Valley an opportunity to watch movies from their automobiles, Shankweiler's served as a landing strip. "Back in the old barnstorming days," claims former owner Bob Malkames, "the pilots would fly in there for Shankweiler Hotel's famous chicken and waffles dinner." Today, Shankweiler's Drive-In is still open for business and is America's oldest operating drive-in theater.

Soon came The Drive-In Short Reel Theater of Galveston, Texas. Because prospective financial investors were skeptical about proprietor Louis Josserand's proposition, he fashioned an "experimental" drive-in theater to test its popularity. The Short Reel Theater, which featured cartoons, comedies, news reels, and short subjects, was a temporary theater built on a beach. Here, all the cars faced out to sea. Each night, the ramps were graded out of sand before the show, wetted with water, and packed down. This process prevented cars from getting stuck. However, the theater only lasted for twenty days as it was destroyed by a tropical storm and never rebuilt. Obviously, drive-ins would have to be built more permanently on solid ground.

Theaters continued to build at a steady rate across the country, mostly in smaller towns and rural communities. However, the

The Riverside Auto Theatre

Frank Yassenoff built and owned several drive-in theaters, including the Riverside Auto Theatre, in Columbus, Ohio. Skip Yassenoff

On Tuesday, June 25, 1940, Frank Yassenoff opened the Riverside Auto Theatre in Columbus, Ohio, a city which had not previously had a drive-in theater to call its own. However, that theater, which sold tickets for 30 cents each during its first season, did not go without its troubles. "It certainly was a 'pit' by the standards of the day," recalls Frank's son, Skip. "The rest rooms were under the screen. The projection booth was four steps below grade and flooded and people could easily walk in front of the picture and block it. Even the ultra high ramps that were probably terrific in 1940 hung up a lot of the newer cars."

Yassenoff made what improvements he could. Like many early theaters, the Riverside opened with large horns on top of the screen, which in turn projected the sound to patrons; complaint came in from several surrounding neighborhoods. Determined to maintain a good rapport with the community, Yassenoff scrambled to come up with an alternate sound system. On August 17, 1940, not more than two months after opening, the local newspaper said the Riverside offered "speakers at every other car." The very next week, the same paper promoted "individual speakers" at each car. Yassenoff was known for always being at the forefront of the drive-in theater business.

He even went so far as to install the first in-car heaters in a Columbus drive-in. As a result, that theater did more business in the winter than it did in the summer during the early days.

Each night Yassenoff would bring in a crew of young boys to help with maintenance, directing traffic, and pulling wagons full of popcorn and bottles of soda. Of course, this was before it was possible to mix fountain drinks, as later concession stands would do. Yassenoff always ran a good business and put on a quality show.

In all, Yassenoff built five drive-ins and acquired one. He was also involved in the ownership of theaters in Kentucky, Ohio, and West Virginia. Today, his son Skip owns Rainbow Theaters, which still operates three drive-ins in central Ohio, none of which are the originals that Yassenoff built.

first major city to open a drive-in theater was Los Angeles. The Pico Drive-In Theatre began welcoming southern California customers in September of 1934, much to the dismay of its inventor. Hollingshead had a difficult time enforcing his patent. While a few owners did sign licensing agreements and provide him with the proper share of box office receipts, others simply disregarded the patent. In fact, Park-In Theaters went to court many times over the matter, but ultimately The First Circuit Court of Appeals determined the subject matter of the patent was not patentable and stated, "This arcuate arrangement of parking stalls in a lot is obviously only an addition to automobiles of the conventional arrangement of seats in a theater employed since ancient times...There is nothing inventive in adapting the old arcuate arrangement of seats in a theater to automobiles in a parking lot as the

A woman stands outside her car at the 8-Mile Drive-In near Detroit, Michigan, in 1938. The roads that run east and west outside of Detroit are marked as miles from the center of downtown. Hence, this theater, which is located on 8-Mile Road, was named the 8-Mile Drive-In.
Archive Photos

An early advertisement for Frank Yassenoff's theater, the first drive-in in Columbus, Ohio. Skip Yassenoff

Self promotion was a key to any good business in the late-1930s. Handmade signs were often used to lure customers into the drive-in theater. In addition to the variety of hand-painted signs and posters that exhibitors created, a showman occasionally received advertising slicks to be used in conjunction with a studio film. Here, two employees of the Riverside Auto Theatre hang a studio sign for the new show. Ralph Bieber

means to achieve horizontal pointing." Hollingshead appealed his patent to the United States Supreme Court on two separate occasions. Both petitions were denied and Hollingshead never did collect the royalties that he felt were rightfully his.

By the late 1930s, a handful of drive-ins were created around the countryside. It truly was a business for the entrepreneur at heart—the dreamer. Farmers converted unused pasture land into theaters, and local businessmen constructed makeshift drive-ins on cheap property at the outskirts of town. With Hollingshead's patent ineffective, there was essentially no law; if an owner could find a way to build the theater cheaper, no one was stopping him. Sound and picture quality tended to suffer as a rule, yet people flocked to these crude theaters. A new icon was beginning to take its form.

Frank Yassenoff hired students at the drive-in to help with concession sales, parking, and other duties. Shown here, clad in custom apparel, are his happy helpers. Ralph Bieber

In the drive-in's early days, most snack bars were not organized to serve hundreds of patrons during the short intermission time, so many owners hired young workers to go from car to car peddling homemade foods. Here, a young man sells a box of popcorn at the drive-in. Ralph Bieber

Prints of movies weren't easy to come by in those early days. Charles A. Richter, the owner of the first permanent drive-in theater in Texas (simply called The Texas Drive-In Theatre), located in Corpus Christi, is an operator who had trouble with major film distributors. The distributors told him that the American people would never accept the idea of sitting in one's car to watch a movie. For this reason, film distribution was often left up to the owner. It was generally expected that an owner would drive great distances to get new movies each week. At the time, no delivery company provided service in these remote areas and shipping was left up to the owner. Arrangements were made, often with a distant indoor theater owner, where a studio would leave an extra print at the indoor theater, and the drive-in owner would come and pick it up.

Early theatrical promotion was not always so obvious. Before the days of advertising

companies, bus stop posters, and billboards, independent theater owners were expected to promote their own shows. Many theater owners began to construct signs, posters, and other makeshift advertising tools intended to lure customers. Even with an item as simple as a marquee that boasted the nightly show, a theater owner would most likely create each letter himself.

By the early 1940s, the drive-in was becoming well established, with approximately 100 theaters existing in 1942. Soon, leisure was forgotten, and Americans began to focus on defending their country. Drive-in growth came to a sudden and complete stop.

Nevertheless, operating theaters continued to see a steady business as they supported their country. Drive-ins backed the war effort by adding a the federally imposed defense tax to their ticket prices. In other instances, when drive-in theaters were located in close proximity to defense plants, the theaters would hold late-night shows for the plant workers, some starting as late as 1:00 am. and ending at 3:45. Business, for the most part, remained fair through the war years. However, it wouldn't be until after World War II that such rapid growth could continue, and when it did, no one could have anticipated its magnitude. The greatest years were yet to come.

Dedication to the Ballyhoo

Early theater owners frequently created their own promotional signs and banners; however, they occasionally had a little help from corporations. As this photograph shows, patrons could enjoy a refreshing Coca-Cola at the Beaches Drive-In in Jacksonville, Florida. In fact, Coca-Cola was the primary refreshment the theater sold. As the story goes, the Coca-Cola Company would travel from town to town offering a theater a fresh coat of paint. In exchange for this generosity, the theater owner was required to advertise Coca-Cola on the back of the screen tower. Such "free advertisements" were soon plastered on drive-ins across the country. Ironically, the faded Coca-Cola advertisement is about the only image left at this abandoned theater today. Although soda was the most popular refreshment served at the Beaches Drive-In during its early days, its owner eventually found he had another marketable commodity—food. However, the ballyhoo surrounding the concession stand at the theater would not take off until the late 1940s. Early theaters sold only coffee, soda, and popcorn. Anything more simply required too much preparation.

The Beaches Drive-In, whose screen tower was constructed entirely of concrete block, still wears the advertisement painted by the Coca-Cola Company.

The Chalk Hill Drive-In opened its gates to the public on Friday, July 4, 1941. It was the second outdoor theater to open in Dallas, Texas. Owned and operated by W.G. Underwood and Claude Ezell, the theater came to be known for its elaborate neon artwork that graced the back of the screen tower. Murals such as this would soon become an important part of many drive-in theaters. Steve Fitch

One shortage that Americans did not face was movies! As this 1942 advertisement attests, Hollywood's best were continuing to grace the screens of drive-in theaters that were able to survive gas rationing and other wartime difficulties.
Brian Butko

Beat the Heat!
... ENJOY THE SHOW OUT-OF-DOORS

DRIVE-IN Theatre

SIT IN YOUR CAR..
See and Hear the Movies!

ATTENTION! VICTORY WORKERS NOW! A COMPLETE LATE SHOW AT 1 A.M. EVERY SATURDAY NIGHT CONTINUOUS FROM DUSK UNTIL 3:45 A.M. COME DIRECTLY FROM WORK DRESS AS YOU PLEASE! MAKE IT A PARTY! BRING YOUR CO-WORKERS! SMOKE! COME OR GO AT ANYTIME

BROOKPARK RD. OPP AIRPORT

During the war, this drive-in owner simply closed the theater and left. The onset of World War II prohibited the building of any new drive-in theaters and left others idle, waiting for the war to end. Ralph Bieber

This drive-in theater advertisement was geared toward the Victory Defense Plant workers. During World War II, it was quite common for theaters to offer late-night shows for those working the odd shifts at defense plants across the country. Brian Butko

29

CHAPTER 2

FIRST FEATURE 1945 to 1955

The decade following the Second World War was like no other time in the history of America. Families were reunited. Families were started. Employment was available, and for the first time everyone went to work—not for the government or the war effort—but for themselves. And they had money—money to buy houses, appliances, and radios. They also had money to buy America's most prized possessions—*cars!*

The car was the ultimate expression of freedom, and auto manufacturers operated around the clock to keep up with the demand for new cars. Highways became crowded as more people were working, taking vacations, and going on Sunday drives. Postwar prosperity nurtured new enterprises, and many found the overloaded American road the perfect place to start a new business and take advantage of traveling motorists. Souvenir shops, gas stations, and drive-in restaurants were springing to life everywhere, but the drive-in theater grew the most significantly.

Everyone enjoyed taking the movie-going experience outside. "Millions of the men and women who were in the Armed Forces and to whom outdoor life appeals, together with many additional millions of factory and office workers who are anxious to take their evening entertainment out of doors in nature's own air-conditioning, are the people who desire to enjoy their movies surrounded by good, clean, fresh air which is untainted by the odors of peanuts, garlic, onions, perspiration, and other

Nearly complete, this theater's screen tower features an empty backside for an artist's mural. These murals, which generally featured images of the local region, not only covered the otherwise empty space, but tied the theater to the surrounding community. Corgan Architects

In 1950, days before its opening, the massive screen tower is raised at the Starlite Drive-In in Montrose, Colorado. Pamela Friend

Eager patrons gather long before showtime to enjoy the outdoors at the Route 45 Drive-In located in Berlinsville, Pennsylvania. Notice that families are arriving early to socialize and take advantage of the twilight sky. After the war, the drive-in theater proved to be a wonderful venue for families and friends to get together. Oliver Mummey

Jack Corgan—
The Drive-In's Legendary Designer

Originally an indoor theater designer, Jack Corgan became a well-known architect of drive-ins in the early 1940s and continued to build drive-ins through the boom years. However, contractors weren't always ready to jump on the bandwagon. Corgan recalls, "They found the drive-in design and layout too unusual, so they didn't want to touch it. We ended up doing the sitework ourselves." To construct large screen towers, he turned to

an architectural method used heavily in the farm belt. "We built a lot of towers the same way as grain elevators using the slip form method. We would pour concrete into a slip that was about 6 feet high. And then we would add another on top of that. That's how it went from the ground up."

However, building the tower was only one obstacle. Corgan also had to create a road design that didn't cause traffic jams while customers waited to pay. "Ideally, a piece of property for a drive-in was 15 acres or more shaped like a rectangle. Our goal was to have enough space for 30 or 40 cars without backing up the traffic on the main road. But sometimes that wasn't possible, because the property we built on was too small or irregularly shaped." By the time Corgan retired in 1980, he had over 75 drive-in theaters to his credit.

Architect Jack Corgan originally designed indoor movie palaces. However, he added drive-in theaters to his repertoire when the demand for new ozoners increased in the late 1940s. Corgan Architects

The slick, sharp lines of the Ventura Drive-In gave motorists a feeling of motion. Dynamic angles and sharp curves were an integral part of many theaters designed by S. Charles Lee. The sketch shows what the client, James Edward, Jr., had envisioned prior to construction of his theater. Department of Special Collections, University of California Los Angeles

Six tons of steel are hoisted into place by a mobile crane. This 62-foot-high tower was used at the Airport Drive-In in Little Falls, Minnesota, the hometown of Charles Lindbergh.

This still from a Filmack Studios drive-in trailer welcomed patrons to movies under the stars. Filmack/Mark Bialek

After World War II, the drive-in theater industry saw its greatest boom in business. In this 1948 photo, a technique known as "stran-steel framing" is used to construct an outdoor movie screen owned by Drive-In Theatres, Inc. of Montgomery, Alabama.

man-made or created smells," wrote George M. Peterson, a theater owners' representative during the postwar boom. "These persons prefer to enjoy their movies in practically the same privacy in which they enjoy reading the evening newspaper in their own homes. These persons are the nucleus of the comparatively new branch of the picture industry which is growing to undreamed-of proportions."

Before the onslaught of television, the drive-in theater offered families and couples a private in-home-style entertainment experience. This meant great growth for the entertainment business, and the drive-in theater came out of hibernation. No longer was it mom and pop hanging a sheet in the tree on the back forty and charging admission. The new theaters were built to last. One individual who

The Pike Drive-In illustrates the great effort that was put into creating murals. This particular design flashed various neon lights; when operating it would appear that the cowboy was getting ready to throw his lasso. Such elaborate neon work cost about $1.50 per foot. Dick V. Mitchell, Texas Sign Company

was highly involved in the designing and building of these theaters was S. Charles Lee. Lee had been designing movie palaces since 1910, but quickly moved to designing elaborate outdoor theaters with great attention to detail. He would frequently combine a theater's facade with its marquee. This fusion helped create an intricate billboard, which advertised the venue as well as the movie playing. Another strategy was to incorporate sharp angles and drastic

lines that gave the theater a sense of movement. All of these design techniques were intended to attract the motoring public.

The focal point of any drive-in theater is the screen tower. Elaborate murals were painted on the side of the screen tower that faced the highway. Most of the time these murals tied into the iconography of the region. The Pike Drive-In in Texas had a cowboy twirling a neon lasso. The Circle, near Baylor University, featured the

school's mascot, a bear, running through a stadium. The Cowtown Drive-In, located in a progressive ranching community, featured a huge steer looking out into the countryside. The people commissioned to create these murals went to great lengths to illustrate some aspect of the community. And it worked—everyone was going to the drive-in.

Between 1946 and 1953, 2,976 drive-ins were built. Because of the heavy publicity surrounding this boom, the drive-in began to receive various slang nicknames in newspapers and trade papers. Some of these names included; "fresh air exhibitors," "outdoorers," "open air operators," "underskyers," "rampitoriums," "mudholes," "cow pastures," and "under-the-stars emporiums." Nevertheless, the nickname that would end up sticking through the years was "ozoner."

Growing Pains

As the drive-in theater gained in popularity and number, it underwent continual change and refinement to remain competitive. Owners wanted to attract as many people as possible, and after accomplishing that, they strived to provide a pleasant experience so those same people would come again. Some difficulties were resolved; others were not.

One problem that continually plagued the ozoner was plain and simple—bugs. Many theaters were located in areas that were pleasant to the eye, but much too hospitable to mosquitoes and other pestiferous insects. One solution was the Car Net, a thin scrim that fit over the frame of the window. This allowed the driver to roll down the window yet not be attacked by hungry bugs. The manufacturer found that this type of item sold

The El Rancho Drive-In in sunny Sacramento, California, incorporates an art moderne style, an adaptation of the 1930s art deco. Sacramento Public Library

best with families that had a sleeping tot in the back seat. Unfortunately, the Car Net didn't solve the problem, so theater owners turned to chemicals. Many would hire pilots to fumigate the theater much like farmers crop dust fields. However, a more common and perhaps less-expensive method incorporated fogging trucks. A theater owner might hire "fogging and dusting" services to come in and spray the lot at intervals of approximately

10 days. The trucks sprayed an oil-based compound called DDT. If a family so wished, they could even have the entire car fumigated with the pesticide. Surprisingly, moviegoers were offended by the strong kerosene-like smell of the spray, not the chemical DDT itself. The carcinogenic poison was officially banned by the United States government in 1972, and swatting mosquitoes is still an ongoing tradition at any drive-in theater.

After World War II, theater owners were still facing the problem of providing patrons with quality sound without offending nearby neighbors. Complaints were putting theater owners under pressure and, as a result, various methods were devised to help cut down excess sound. An early attempt, best illustrated by the San-Val Drive-In, in Burbank, California, provided each car with a rudimentary speaker that sat right in front of the car. In addition, each row of speakers could be turned on or off, allowing the theater to shut down the rows not used on a slow night and thus reducing the subsequent noise pollution. These speakers were all mastered by one volume control, which was located in the projec-

tion booth. A signal system was devised between the ticket girl and the projection room whereby, if a truck or train passed and drowned out the soundtrack, the ticket girl could alert the projectionist to turn up the volume. Cutting-edge technology like this would cost an owner approximately $5,000.

Another system, developed by W.G. Underwood, who co-owned a string of ozoners in Texas, developed a system called "Sound in the Ground." In this case, patrons pulled their car over a speaker which was planted in the ground. A metal grate, much like a manhole cover, protected the speaker which rumbled the sound up through the floorboards. Again, this system had no volume

This fogging rig, owned by A.M. Cochran of Montclair, New Jersey, served a number of drive-in theaters within a 100-mile radius. By spraying an oil-based DDT insecticide over the entire theater lot, owners hoped to rid themselves of mosquitoes and other small insects. It was generally thought that such spraying was most effective at 10-day intervals.

An advertisement from a Kansas City newspaper goes all out to promote the big-star movies playing at the local drive-in. But it doesn't stop there. The spot also hypes various kiddie attractions with hopes of bringing out a family audience. Andy Hanson

An alternative to fogging the drive-in lot was the use of a window screen. The screen pictured here, known as the Gary Insect Guard, or "GIG," was just large enough to stretch over the window. The screen would supposedly keep bugs out, while allowing fresh air and smoke to ventilate. The screens could then be rolled up and kept in the glove box.

DOWNS DRIVE-IN THEATRE
CLEVELAND, O.
JACK K. VOGEL

control and simply did not solve the problem.

It wasn't until 1946 that RCA introduced the drive-in speaker as we know it today. Although the company developed the system in 1941, the war put a delay on the construction of new drive-ins and the production of such a device. These small speaker boxes would pump the tinny sound right into one's automobile, and the volume of each box could be controlled separately, putting a halt to the complaints of neighbors losing sleep.

Along with the application of improved sound quality came the various promotions for which the drive-in is known. Ozoners tried to attract more moms by offering "laundry-while-you-wait." In Memphis, Tennessee, Barney Woolner put together such a service. Here, a housewife could give her laundry to an attendant as she entered the drive-in and

pick it up—laundered and dried—when the film was over. Bottle warmers were added so parents could tend to the young fries while enjoying the movie. At the Westbury Drive-In Theatre in Nassau County, Long Island, New York, a supervised nursery was provided, and a telephone service—for the professionally minded businessman—was available. Other events and contests at the Westbury included 25-cent pony rides, baby parades, slipper kicking, pie throwing, beautiful child pageants, and talent shows. Many of these activities took place between the bottom of the screen and the front row of cars. Awards, generally tickets to next week's show, were given away as prizes. Paul Petersen, a theater executive, explained the logic behind such promotions by saying, "Unlike the conventional theater, which primarily sells its screen

By 1951, the patronage of drive-ins was exceeding that of indoor theaters, which had sharply declined. Here, a packed drive-in theater crowd eagerly watches from the comfort of their cars as the drama plays out upon the screen. UPI/Bettmann

The Downs Drive-In, shown in this Jack Vogel rendering, gave a hint of the futuristic look that was soon coming to the Midwest. Mark Bialek

41

A concept that never caught on was underground sound projection. Theater owner W.G. Underwood shows off the new concept, which piped sound underground and up through grilled manhole covers. The sound would then blast through the floorboards of the automobile and into the car. Often muffled and difficult to hear, this system simply was not very practical. Fort Worth *Star-Telegram* Photograph Collection, Special Collections Division, The University of Texas at Arlington Libraries, Arlington, Texas

attraction, drive-in theater advertising must concentrate on the full evening's inexpensive entertainment it offers to the entire family, of which movies are only a part." Advertisements would frequently offer flowers for the ladies or coupons for a free gallon of gasoline. Local service stations would often participate and donate the gasoline, knowing very well that the customers would continue to fill up after using the coupon. Oftentimes the patrons would purchase oil or some type of snack while their cars were being refueled. The stations couldn't really lose money.

Theater owners offered all kinds of offbeat services and extravaganzas. Everything from jump-starting cars, fireworks shows, live

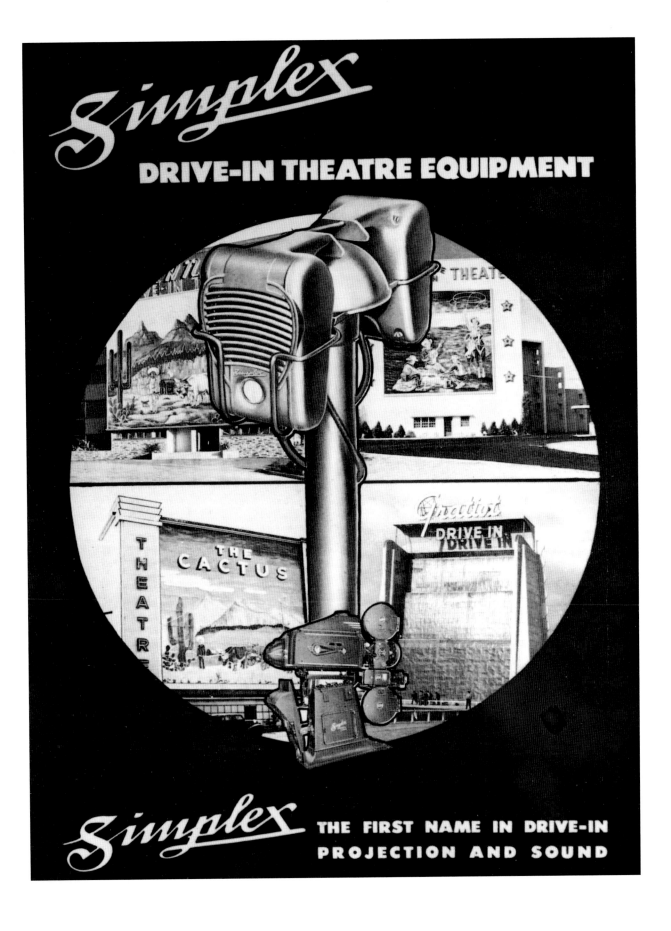

A matchbook cover for the Route 110 Drive-In on Long Island, New York. Matchbooks like this were often used as advertising materials in the drive-in industry. The message would act as a subtle reminder of the theater each and every time the smoker lit a cigarette. Brian Butko

Opposite, top left
Many times, a drive-in theater would publish a brochure to promote its opening. The cover of this folder promotes the drive-in as a romantic and glamorous environment in which to enjoy a film. Michael Witzel

Opposite, bottom
The Hi-Way Drive-In was one of many theaters that jumped in on early promotional stunts to supplement movies and snacks. Aside from offering a film featuring the voice of Bing Crosby, the advertisement promotes pony rides and a Monkey Village in which the kids could see "real live monkeys." Andy Hanson

music, dancing, and car stunts, to dancing monkeys and boxing matches were all held within the property lines of the drive-in. It was the sizzle that sold tickets at the drive-ins, not the movies they played.

The Lure of the Lights

One thing early architects did to attract patrons was to incorporate extravagant neon artwork into drive-in murals. As mentioned previously, murals became a way in which drive-ins could connect with their customers. They would reflect the community or region. However, many theaters soon began to detail or outline portions of these murals with neon lacing. The idea was to attract impulse customers, patrons who would otherwise not stop at the drive-in. Because ozoners were typically located along highways at the outskirts of town, owners would attract passing motorists with brilliantly lit neon. The

A 1951 Mercury cruises past a Texas drive-in located near the Mexican border. Notice the !Eva De America! !Fundacion Eva Peron! written on the side of the car and the picture of Eva Peron in the back window. The writing translates to "Eva of America! Foundation of Eva Peron!" The motorists were most likely members of a non-profit organization for Eva Peron and were raising money to help underprivileged people in America. Little did the family know that the actress Madonna would make Eva Peron more famous today than she was in 1951. Henry Ford Museum and Greenfield Village

Dominic Frangiamore, head usher at the Whitestone Bridge Drive-in in New York City, adjusts a speaker for Mr. and Mrs. Harry Karst. There was a separate speaker for each car. The Whitestone Bridge Drive-In was one of two outdoor theaters in the New York area in 1951. UPI/Bettmann

bright colors would stand out against the twilight sky and offer a cheerful invitation to travelers. Companies such as Poblocki and Sons, Wagner Sign Company, Texas Neon Sign Company, and Federal Sign Company were only a few of the businesses commissioned to create this artwork.

Not surprisingly, the drive-in industry widely supported the use of such elaborate neon. "Being a branch of show business, it is important that the theaters SHOW the public what they have to offer," explained a 1956 Theater Owners Guide. "The most direct method of achieving this is by the use of marquees. Backs of screen towers, painted with murals or trimmed with bright swirls of neon and mazdas, are converted into imposing facades. Marquee-like structures, towers, panels, and all sorts of ingeniously designed lighting mounts serve as attention-getters and distinctive signatures." Not only did the beautiful neon attract patrons from across the state, but it made an attempt to represent cultures from

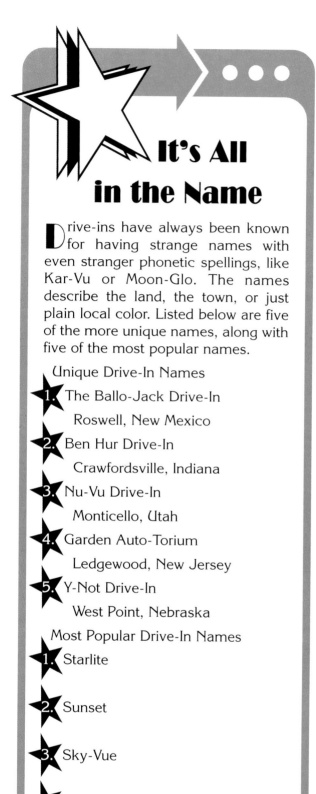

It's All in the Name

Drive-ins have always been known for having strange names with even stranger phonetic spellings, like Kar-Vu or Moon-Glo. The names describe the land, the town, or just plain local color. Listed below are five of the more unique names, along with five of the most popular names.

Unique Drive-In Names

1. The Ballo-Jack Drive-In
   Roswell, New Mexico
2. Ben Hur Drive-In
   Crawfordsville, Indiana
3. Nu-Vu Drive-In
   Monticello, Utah
4. Garden Auto-Torium
   Ledgewood, New Jersey
5. Y-Not Drive-In
   West Point, Nebraska

Most Popular Drive-In Names

1. Starlite
2. Sunset
3. Sky-Vue
4. Drive-In
5. Hi-Way

*Eager patrons enter through the
fancy ticket booth at their local
New York outdoor movie theater.*
UPI/Bettmann

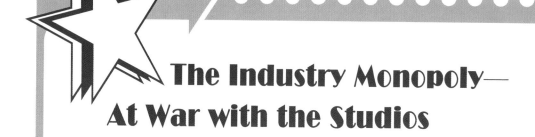

The Industry Monopoly—
At War with the Studios

Drive-in theaters have long battled with major film studios over booking quality, top-rate movies. The major studios simply dominated the film industry and didn't want to cheapen their image by releasing movies to outdoor theaters. Such film factories included Warner Brothers, MGM, 20th Century Fox, United Artists, Columbia, Universal, RKO, and Paramount. These studios owned their own theaters, which allowed them to make, distribute, and exhibit their own product. In 1949, the courts ruled that such a practice was a monopoly on the film industry, and over the years, it was broken up. Nevertheless, the majors still controlled the product coming out of Hollywood and still determined the price of film rental. The studios made the price of first-run features so expensive for drive-ins that only older features were affordable. "The first film at the drive-in was three years old and cost us $400 for four days," claimed Hollingshead, regarding the high cost of rentals. "The last time the film had run was in a little South Camden movie [house] that paid $20 a week for it."

Drive-in theater promotions and admission policies angered Hollywood. Studios disliked promotions such as "children under 12 admitted free," or "buck night," in which every car, regardless of how many passengers it had, got in for only $1. Because ozoner profits relied largely on concession stand revenue, such promotions were common. Hollywood was fuming. MGM president William Rodgers felt drive-ins represented unfair trade within the film community. Rodgers voiced his concern in an address to the Theater Owners of America. "I refer here to those types of operations who have free admission; those who advertise and invite busloads of patrons to attend the drive-in theaters at a specified price for the entire busload, and others who subordinate the attractions and level their sights on the development of their business on concessions. We do not believe that these offenders are entitled to the same availability of our product as those drive-in theaters that operate on a legitimate business."

Unfortunately, the ozoner always found itself at the whim of distributors. Product was eventually made available on a "percentage only" basis, meaning that theaters simply paid the studios a percentage of total ticket sales, and at one point, these percentages got as high as 35 percent. In the end, theaters were still left with unwanted and outdated products.

across the nation. "The imaginatively designed attraction boards and novel lighting displays of the outdoor theaters have transplanted bits of Times Square glamour along highways winding from the historical New England countryside, through the waving Kansas wheatfields to the Pacific. The showman's touch in dressing up the front of the outdoor theater in an inviting manner is a factor of considerable import in the phenomenal growth of the drive-in from a roadside curiosity to a vital component of the entertainment industry in a span of two decades."

Architect Jack Corgan recalls, "We had to worry about vandals getting to the neon...so we wanted to put it high enough so no one could easily reach it." And as far as vandals are concerned, this worked. However, as the years

The Olympic Drive-In of Los Angeles, California, was one of the earliest ozoners to offer entertainment to integrated audiences. The theater, which was originally located on Pico Boulevard, and was called the Pico Drive-In, was picked up and moved to the Olympic Boulevard site. Regardless of location, the theater was the first outdoor movie venue in all of Los Angeles. Pacific Theatres

An interior view of the Olympic Drive-In. Notice the crude speaker system, one of the many flash-in-the-pan solutions that was devised to cut down on noise pollution at outdoor theaters. Pacific Theatres

Drive-In Movies

Coral Way—Con't W. from 1-C	32-33	
7080 Coral Way, Miami		
Le Jeune Auto Park Theatre 6-G	22-25	
1201 N.W. 42nd Ave. Miami		
LIBCITY (colored)	9-C	22-25
6900 N.W. 22nd Ave., Miami		
Miami Drive-In Theater 10-B	22-25	
705 N.W. 81st St., Miami		
Tropicaire Drive-In Theater		
Con't W. from 1-E	32.33	
7751 Bird Road. Miami		
Twenty-Seventh Ave.		
Drive-In	8-A	22-25
2700 N.W. 87th St.. Miami		
Boulevard Drive-In Theater 8-D	28-29	
14311 Biscayne Blvd.. N. Miami		
Dixie Drive-In Theatre		
Perrine	See map page 20-21	

Shown here is an excerpt from the 1953 edition of Griffin's Guide to Greater Miami, a publication that was handed out to those visiting the Miami area. Notice that one of the eight drive-in theaters is the LIBCITY, an outdoor theater that was built for African Americans. Other such drive-ins were the Lincoln Drive-In in Fort Myers, Florida, which opened in 1953, and Bob's Drive-In in Shreveport, Louisiana. Brian Butko

A Starlite Drive-In advertisement in the Dallas Express, a paper with a primarily black readership, advertises its current lineup of movies. The theater boasted of offering entertainment that was the "Southwest's Finest For Colored Americans." Dallas Public Library

The Drive-In Theatre, located in Chincoteague, Virginia, was yet another outdoor theater that welcomed African American patrons. In fact, by the mid-1950s, integrated drive-ins had become quite popular.

At The Sunset Drive-In in Hamburg, Arkansas, separate seating was provided for those of color.

passed, parts of these signs would burn out or break, giving the theaters a broken-down look. And maintenance was expensive. Trying to preserve their image, theaters would strip down the neon and simply repaint the back of the tower. Occasionally, the mural would be repainted, but for the most part, these renovations took place in the late 1960s, well after the fascination with outdoor theaters had passed. Most owners would simply strip the neon and paint a solid color on the back of the screen tower. If any neon was salvaged, it would be the name of the theater, which would still light up across the top of the screen.

Construction of new theaters continued. Architects like Jack Vogel and S. Charles Lee were gainfully employed designing new drive-ins. At the same time, between 1948 and 1954, the number of indoor theaters declined by over 130,000 screens. Everyone loved the ozoner. Businesses began to cater to the needs of outdoor theaters. Companies made devices like in-car heaters, cool-air blowers, split rail fences, rain-away canopies, and hand-held fogging machines for those pesky mosquitoes. One entrepreneur, hoping to cash in on the popularity of the outdoor theater, even went so far as to redesign the drive-in. In his theater, each car had its own screen. The concept, known as the Auto-scope, combined the luxuries of the outdoor movie theater with television. Although the

Although the movies shown at drive-ins might not have been first-run status, motorists cruised out to see them anyway. Automobiles were a status symbol, and drive-ins provided a meeting place for proud owners.

owner even tried to change the name to "Cinema 360" to sound more elaborate, the Autoscope never reached the popularity of the bigger, more traditional drive-in screen.

Ignoring the meek imitation, the true drive-in marched on. Designs continued to get more and more elaborate. No longer was an old wooden screen tower enough. Now, owners tried to give their theaters themes. Some built them to look like Southern homes; others were constructed to resemble colonial mansions. Water shows were installed in the front of some theaters with synchronized dancing water fountains. The Gratiot Drive-In in Detroit, Michigan, and the Kallet Drive-In in Syracuse,

As the outdoor theater business continued to boom, many developers proposed ambitious community centers like this one. Here, an architect illustrates plans for a center that would feature a sports arena, a shopping center, a 1,000-seat indoor theater, a 100-room hotel, a 46-room motel, and a 750-car drive-in. The complex, which was never built, was to remain open year around.

Harvey Elliott, manager of the Whitestone Bridge Drive-In, in greater New York, spoke confidently of the drive-in in 1949. "Fad! Let me tell you that the drive-in theater is no fad; this is a country on wheels. We like to eat on wheels, telephone on wheels, and listen to the radio on wheels. Why not see a movie on wheels?" Here, moviegoers pack his Whitestone Bridge Drive-In, one of two theaters in the greater New York area. The theater proved to be highly successful and popular with New Yorkers who previously confined themselves to the bright lights of Broadway and local neighborhood theaters. The Whitestone Drive-In could accommodate 1,200 automobiles. UPI/Bettmann

The Westview Drive-In was another theater that featured animated neon opposite the screen. On this mural, the flashing lights would give the feeling that the cowboy was about to throw his lasso. Such animation was designed to pull moviegoers off the nearby highway and into the theater. Jimmie Willis 1948, from the James Jasek collection

New York, both featured huge waterfalls on the back of the screen tower. Patrons would come early to stand in front of the screen tower and have the water cascade down in front of them. The cool mist felt good in the summer. It was the next best thing to Niagara Falls—and without the cost of an airplane ticket.

The drive-in theater industry as a whole was getting bigger by the day. And though it had more muscle as an organized effort than

ever before, it wasn't powerful enough to generate any significant support from other industries and government. As an example, theater owners once banded together to lobby the large auto makers. Their hope was to convince automobile manufacturers to halt production of the tinted window, which darkened the drive-in screen's image. In addition, theater operators wanted Detroit to make the front windshield bigger, for better drive-in viewing. Unfortu-

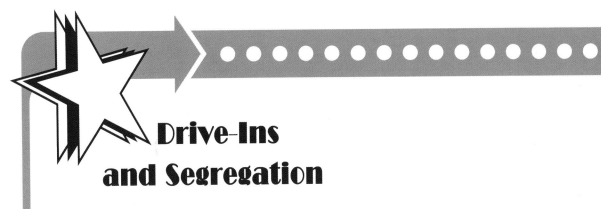

Drive-Ins and Segregation

By 1951, many drive-ins were accommodating everyone, including the African American community. Although segregation was not common in many parts of the country, theaters such as the Olympic Drive-In in Los Angeles led the way in providing entertainment to all people, regardless of race. Ruth Lloyd, an African American who moved to Los Angeles at the age of 16 with her family, remembers the drive-in as being a "real nice place to go." Lloyd used to attend the Olympic Drive-In two times a week with her male friend as early as 1951.

In the South, where segregation was quite prevalent, many drive-ins had separate entrances and seating areas for African Americans. The Sunset Drive-In of Hamburg, Arkansas, was one such theater. Although colored patrons could sit in their cars just as other guests, separate seating areas were provided at the concession stand. In Richmond, Virginia, The Bellwood Drive-In was a fully segregated theater. Here, the theater was equipped with separate entrances, restrooms, eating facilities, and parking as well. The Lariat Drive-In in Fort Worth, Texas, was built near a new subdivision for the African American community, and the Star-Lite Drive-In in Dallas was a theater intended for colored patrons only. As Dallas resident Jack Coleman remembers, the Star-Lite Drive-In was the place to be. "I remember The Starlite Drive-In Movie Theater opening on Lamar Street just after the war. It was a great place for African Americans at the time, as it was the only drive-in theater we could attend because of segregation." All across the South theaters were being built for the African American community, but in time, all drive-ins became integrated.

The Starview Drive-In was nestled in a lovely wooded area. The theater boasted of having refreshments, golfette, ping-pong, and badminton. Brian Butko

Entryways and landscaping became more elaborate as theaters attempted to change their bleak appearance. This advertisement from the Fence Company of America promoted the benefits of its "showmanship setting" products. Andy Hanson

Opposite, top left
This in-car heater was only one of many heating devices that attempted to keep moviegoers warm in the winter. Because theaters were already limited to nighttime business hours, cold weather conditions cut drastically into their already short season. Theater owner Wilfred Smith tried to appeal to his customers' macho instincts. Thinking that patrons might like to brag to their friends about seeing a movie while there was frost on the windows, he flashed pep talks on the screen that read: "You hardy folks may be interested to know that the temperature is now twenty-five degrees. We have always been of the opinion that real drive-in patrons would attend during the winter, just as they bundle up to go to a football game or ice-skating. Pass along the good news that we will be here all winter, bringing you top entertainment."

FENCING IN RUSTIC
THE "Showmanship Setting" FOR DRIVE-IN THEATRES

STOCKADE FENCING: Stockade fencing designed for open-air theatres—made of hand-peeled split white cedar posts with three full round stringers fitting into mortised line posts for easy erection. Factory fabricated sections 6'10" high and 6'10" wide. When installed the over-all dimensions are approximately 7' high and 7' wide. Weight: approximately 150# per section.

TICKET OFFICE AND REFRESHMENT STANDS: Rugged Michigan log buildings for ticket office and refreshment stands. Amazingly inexpensive and easily assembled from factory-built precision sections.

BUMPER FENCING: Knife-peeled, full, round rail fence available in one to four rail heights. Easily assembled into mortised line posts.

RUSTIC IS BOX-OFFICE — CREATES ATMOSPHERE THAT FITS INTO NATURAL SURROUNDINGS OF THE OUTDOOR THEATRE

(1) LOW COST: Factory fabrication eliminates the necessity of skilled workers for installation.

(2) EASY INSTALLATION: All that is necessary is to place the tenoned ends of the sections into the mortised line posts which give rigid support.

(3) DURABILITY: Thoroughly air dried saplings insures fully seasoned pickets that will not shrink or warp after erection. Treated with wood preservative optional.

(4) BEAUTY: Nature's most beautiful and durable wood made exclusively of northern Michigan white cedar, carefully hand-peeled to create the natural effect desired for drive-in theatre landscaping.

(5) IMMEDIATE DELIVERY.

If structures are of unusual size, we also have available loose machine and prepared logs ready for assembly. Literature and prices available on request.

We invite inquiries and will cooperate with open-air theatres, architects, suppliers and builders.

FENCE COMPANY of AMERICA
Sales Office and Showrooms: 608 SO. DEARBORN ST., CHICAGO 5, ILLINOIS
Factory: ESCANABA, MICHIGAN

The Hickory Drive-In displayed a charismatic neon structure that hoped to prompt impulse ticket sales. Steve Fitch

The marquee of the Kallet Drive-In in Syracuse, New York, featured wild dancers and brightly colored bulbs that pointed patrons toward the theater.

When broken or burnt out, neon grids would most likely be stripped and the mural repainted. In many instances, the entire back of the screen tower would be repainted a solid color, leaving only the name of the theater showing at the top. However, in the case of the Bordertown Drive-In, the owner had elected to keep the theater's integrity and let the giant bull stand the test of time. Steve Fitch

nately, both attempts were futile, but the very actions of the theater owners brought respectability to the drive-in theater industry.

Business was booming. Owners were pulling together with new ideas and concepts. Plans were drawn up for various drive-in spin-offs. One such concept was a two-screen, 800-car, indoor drive-in theater resort. It was to have giant ventilation blowers in the roof to pull exhaust from the cars up and out of the building. A two-level foyer around the back of the theater would include a bowling alley, miniature golf course, dancing floor, and several restaurants. Other theaters were designed around lakes where patrons could dock their boats at giant marinas. They could then sit in their boat and watch the movie from the water. And various theaters were built with indoor seating areas at the back of the theater. This allowed those who disliked the automobile experience to relax in the indoor theater. In addition, it allowed the drive-in to double as an indoor theater during the cold winter months.

Although watching a film from the com-

fort of one's own car might sound pleasurable on a cool summer night, it was not so comfortable for those folks in southern states like Alabama, Louisiana, and Florida. To remedy the muggy nights, theater owners came up with various outdoor air-conditioning systems. One early concept was an underground central-air cooling device built into the Lake Worth Drive-In in Lake Worth, Florida. Here, a central air-conditioning system sat at the back of the theater lot. It operated during the film and pumped cool air through asbestos pipes that were laid underground much like the speaker wires for the sound system. A hose, which protruded from the ground, could then be hooked to the driver's-side window allowing cool air to flow into the automobile. However, like most drive-in inventions, the system

Baby-Sitters "Picket" Drive-In

Dick V. Mitchell and the Texas Neon Sign Company

After working in a bomber plant during World War II, Dick V. Mitchell partnered up with Ed McAdams to form the Texas Manufacturing Company, where they created neon signs for local businesses. Over the years, the business continued to grow, and Mitchell soon purchased his partner's share in the company, thus forming the Texas Neon Sign Company. "Dick was a great man," recalls past employee Temple Hall. "He was a real artist with neon and truly created neon spectaculars."

Mitchell's skill as a glass blower was evident in the signs he created. He was responsible for the creation of several great drive-in neon murals, including the Pike Drive-In and Belknap Drive-In theaters in Texas. At these theaters, extensive neon worked as a type of animation in which flashing parts of the sign implied movement.

But the signs didn't go without their share of strange problems. "There's a bird's nest in ole' Clem's ear!" That's what a service man told Temple Hall after a routine check. "I had no idea what on earth he was talking about. Then he went on to explain, 'The cowboy on the Belknap Drive-In mural, ole' Clem, well, he's got a bird's nest in his ear. Shorted it out. We need to fix it!'"

Actually, birds loved drive-in neon. Not only was its surface perfect for building nests, it was close to the nightly food supply of popcorn and peanuts that were dropped in the theater lot. But birds and nests cause damage. As in the case of ole' Clem, repairs would then have to be made and maintenance costs soared. Over the years such costs became prohibitive to drive-in operators. The new technology of plastics and fluorescent tubing would soon replace the elaborate neon created by the craftsmen of the 1950s.

Years later, the Texas Neon Sign Company was purchased and later closed. Temple Hall, who worked with Dick V. Mitchell until Dick retired in 1974, still finds employment in the neon field. She is employed by Day-Night Signs in Granbury, Texas, home of the Brazos Drive-In.

The members of the renowned Texas Manufacturing Company. Shown from left to right are Kent Mitchell (sales representative), Dick V. Mitchell, (co-founder and owner), Gloria McCarty (secretary), and Ed McAdams (co-founder). The company was busy producing "neon spectaculars" for indoor and outdoor theaters alike until Dick V. Mitchell retired in 1974. Dick V. Mitchell, Texas Sign Company

A delighted customer pays the ticket lady. Note the price in the window, only 65 cents for an adult admission. UPI/Bettmenn

In this photo from 1952, neon lights were used extensively at the Beverly Drive-In Theatre on the entrance canopy and sign. A.J. Roquevert

Occasionally, when funds weren't available for elaborate murals or neon, the obvious was simply stated. Standard Oil Collection, University of Louisville Photographic Archives

The Autoscope— An Offshoot of the Ozoner

During the heyday of the drive-in, it seemed everyone wanted a piece of the action. And as Americans have learned, sometimes being different can give one a competitive edge. Applying this philosophy, Tom Smith and Bert Crowley of Buffalo, Missouri, came up with something very different. On August 1, 1954, their Autoscope opened. It was billed as the "world's first private screen theater." With this type of theater, 150 to 200 cars were arranged in a wagon wheel-like circle with a single projection booth and snack bar in the center. A "fly's eye lens" was the heart of Smith's invention. The projection system reflected the image off a series of mirrors, directed it through portholes in the projection building, and then back-projected the image onto the individual 3 x 5-foot screens. "You could say it's rather

Vivian Breshears

At the Autoscope, cars entered a one-way circle and parked in front of a single screen. The snack bar and restrooms were located at the center of the wagon wheel-shaped theater, where the projection booth was also found. AP/Wide World Photos

Co-inventor Bert Crowley shows off his "fly's eye lens," the secret to the Autoscope and multiple projection. Vivian Breshears

crude, but there is no denying that the result is comparable with the best of front-projection, indoors and out," claimed inventor Smith. " I don't think we'll make a million dollars out of this brainchild, but I do think we've got something here."

In an article that was published just before the opening of the theater, Smith's wife said the project could easily become the "theater of tomorrow." The article went on to note that, "these very words have been repeated many times by various men in the motion picture industry." Evidently, the talk stopped there. Although theaters were built in Joplin, Missouri, Albuquerque, New Mexico, Houston, Texas, and Anchorage, Alaska, their existence was fairly short-lived and all are gone today.

did have a major glitch. Because the tubing was laid underground, mice, bugs, and other small critters would frequently crawl inside the coolant's asbestos pipes during the day. When patrons turned on the air-conditioning device, they more than likely had a mouse or another small varmint blown into their lap. Sure, it might sound like an inconvenience, but it's a small price to pay for the luxury of air-conditioning in the great outdoors. With all these grand themes, the theaters continued

to profit and bring in larger crowds, but they weren't all families anymore.

The mid-1950s saw the emergence of the independent teenager. The young shavers who attended the drive-in with their family in the late-1940s now drove to the drive-in with their boyfriends or girlfriends. It was the first time teenagers had affluence. They had money, they had cars, and they wanted to go do something. Why not go to a movie in your car?

The Sidney Lust Drive-In was another theater design penned by architect Jack Vogel. This original drawing shows how the theater was to look upon completion. The actual theater was later built in Beltsville, Maryland. Alterations to Vogel's original concept were made by architect George M. Petersen, who was brought on to finish the design. Mark Bialek

Beltline Drive-In Theatre

Newest and Finest IN WESTERN MICHIGAN

EASY TO REACH

BELTLINE Drive-In THEATRE

OPENS SATURDAY

CONVENIENTLY LOCATED SOUTH BELT LINE AT BURLINGAME

LARGEST PICTURE SCREEN IN MICHIGAN

TILTED FOR PERFECT VISION

MOTIAGRAPH, MIRROPHONIC SOUND EQUIPMENT FOR IN-CAR SPEAKERS

PUSH BUTTON LIGHTS FOR TRAY SERVICE

IT'S FUN FOR THE ENTIRE FAMILY!

Beltline DRIVE-IN Theatre

NOW SHOWING RAIN OR CLEAR

Opening feature: **"RED STALLION"** in TECHNICOLOR with Robert Page

PLUS COLOR CARTOON AND FIRST RUN NEWS

SIT IN THE COMFORT OF YOUR OWN CAR — NO PARKING PROBLEMS — SMOKE, TALK, EAT AT WILL — COME DRESSED AS YOU ARE — WHOLE PARTY CAN SIT TOGETHER — REFRESHMENTS IN YOUR CAR — BRING THE CHILDREN — ELIMINATE BABY-SITTER PROBLEMS — FOR BABIES—FREE BOTTLE-WARMING SERVICE — IDEAL FOR SHUT INS — CHILDREN UNDER 12 FREE

The ozoner offered teens a place to meet and hang out, to get away from their parents. The actual movie wasn't so important. "It was the act of getting to the drive-in," explains author Michael Wallis. "[It was] getting on a clean T-shirt and clean jeans for the night—you've got the car washed, it's all cleaned up, and the radio's all tuned in. Everything's set. Then you go out and maybe you make a pass through the Dog 'n Suds or the Steak'n Shake, and you're seen and you have to be seen and you look for the scosh position up there. I mean, a lot of that *American Graffiti* stuff is true." Of course, then there were those little meetings throughout the night under the yellow neon of the snack bar. Who was with who—? Who wore what? The gossip was always more important than the show.

The drive-in was on fire! Everyone went—families, dates, kids, and parents. Of course, when there's that many people in one place, there's always the opportunity to make more money—especially when everyone's hungry...

This 1950s advertisement illustrates how theater owners promoted their various amenities rather than the featured film. Here, the ad for the grand opening of the Beltline Drive-In Theatre in western Michigan points out not only the large screen, but also the snack bar call button feature, the Motiograph "Mirrophonic" speaker system, and bottle-warming service for infants. Mark Bialek

This postcard shows the Hallandale Drive-In in Hollywood, Florida. Notice the Hollywood Kennel Club race track in the foreground. Many drive-ins were built joining other forms of entertainment. Obviously, in Florida, drive-ins and dog racing went together! Brian Butko

In 1953, the owners of the Kaufman Pike Drive-In had not yet devised a way to keep people from driving in the exit. Sure, the metal tire gate that punctured and ripped tires would soon become quite common, but until then, quick thinking was required. An open exit welcomed accidents and sneak-ins. For this reason, the owners of the Kaufman Pike hired 14-year-old Bobby Butler to take care of their problems. It was Bobby's job to show up at the theater about an hour early. He would then spend about 45 minutes with the owner collecting rocks and broken bricks from the theater lot. Once the theater opened for the night, Bobby took his place hiding in a bush near the exit. If a car tried to sneak in through the exit, it was Bobby's job to throw rocks at the car and try to break its windshield. If he nailed it dead on and smashed the window, rumor was sure to spread through town encouraging others to purchase a ticket as opposed to risking a broken windshield.

This window washer at the Gratiot Drive-In in Detroit, Michigan, worked hard for a tip. As theater amenities grew in the early 1950s, drive-ins across the nation began to employ window washers, who would generally work for tips only. Legend has it that at the Gratiot, on a rainy night, the hired attendants would rub a patron's windshield with a wet sack of Bull Durham. Such a ritual eliminated any distortion caused by the streaking rain.

After a metal tire gate was installed, Bobby's job detail shifted, a promotion of sorts. If a car came in that looked extra heavy, it was his job to pop the trunk and bust any stowaways. However, in those days, girls were known to wear large skirts with petticoats, and kids who had been busted trying to sneak in via the trunk became a bit more devious. For this reason, it was Bobby's job to look under any full skirts and make sure there were no kids hiding beneath the petticoat. It just might be that young Bobby had the best job in town.

Mrs. Jo Jenulis of New Hyde Park, Long Island, New York, found the drive-in perfect for feeding her little boy, Bobby, without having to miss a single scene of the motion picture. Bottle warming became a very common feature at ozoners in the early 1950s as it made it possible for the entire family to enjoy the show. UPI/Bettmann

As time went on, many theater owners became more serious about presentation. This unusual theater in Niles, Michigan, features a stark, downlit illumination, which enhances the fieldstone block in the ticket area. The photograph, which was taken in 1948, also features ushers who wear elaborate uniforms complete with capes, caps, and gloves.

This theater welcomed young and old alike. The middle and back rows were generally used by older couples and people who preferred to see the entire movie. The front rows were occupied by young families that took advantage of several benches for energetic tots. A.J. Roquevert

An early double feature advertisement from 1951. Giveaways, contests, and drawings were common at outdoor theaters.

The drive-in theater knew it had arrived in high society when it was able to grace the cover of the fashionable New Yorker *magazine. The magazine boasted advertisements for airlines, fine clothing, and expensive liquors. The drive-in theater now had impressive company.*

67

Oftentimes, drive-in theaters were used for other purposes. Here, the Austin, Texas, Symphony performs "the world's first drive-in symphony concert at the Chief Drive-In. Some 1,600 people in approximately 400 cars showed up for the Sunday afternoon concert and heard the 65-piece, denim-clad orchestra perform works by Bizet, de Falla, and Strauss. A spot-check of the audience revealed that 58 percent of them had never attended a concert."
UPI/Bettmann

At Home in a Drive-In

In 1947, in the Wasatch Mountains on the eastern edge of Salt Lake City, stood the Motor-Vu Drive-In. However, it was no ordinary theater. The Motor-Vu's owner, Erick C. Peterson, found that he and his family were spending far too much time at the drive-in during its opening season. So they moved a little closer. They built a house inside the screen tower of the drive-in. Peterson explained, "We found that my son Carl and I were up until far into the morning because of the necessity of being at the theater constantly until after it closed for the night, then driving home. Our first season wore us to shadows." Peterson went on to say, "The theater location is such as to provide one of the best view sites in Salt Lake Valley. Others pay premium prices for home building lots with less advantages. We decided we could build a comfortable home with a beautiful view right on the site, and incorporate it into the theater tower so that we could be at home and still at work."

The home featured all the necessities of modern living. It was complete with a living room, a master bedroom, a second bedroom, a kitchen and breakfast nook, a utility room, a reception room, a master bath and powder room, a sound studio, and a theater repair shop. In addition, the theater outside was built with a stage for live music acts to perform before the show.

Several of these "drive-in homes" were built over the years, mostly for added protection. An owner could be at home and know that vandals weren't terrorizing the theater during the day. In fact, Howard T. Chapman of Cowpens, South Carolina, estimated that he saved approximately $175 per month by not hiring a night watchman. His drive-in home had two floors and enough space for 12 rooms. Although many told him the idea of living in a drive-in screen tower was a bit isolated, Chapman defended, "Who else has company in their back yard every single night?"

In the early 1950s, Sue Hargroder, a retired New Orleans theater executive, moved to Hattiesburg, Mississippi, where she and her husband, J.H. Hargroder, built the Beverly Drive-In Theatre. From the beginning, the Beverly was intended to function as a home as well. And in that capacity, it has functioned just fine. In fact, although the theater is now closed, Sue continues to live in the screen tower today! A.J. Roquevert

A rare quiet moment is enjoyed by Howard Chapman and his wife in the kitchen of their drive-in theater home. The home, which was part of the Cherry Hill Drive-in in Cowpens, South Carolina, was constructed circa 1952.

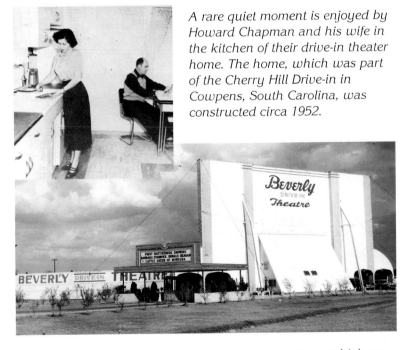

The Beverly Drive-In home included a two-car garage, which can be seen at the far right side of the photo. A.J. Roquevert

CHAPTER 3

INTERMISSION

In early drive-in theaters, the concession stand was never really the focal point of the evening. Patrons expected to go to the ozoner and watch a movie or two. However, soon after the novelty of the outdoor theater wore off, owners turned to other forms of income-generating methods to help keep the theater profitable. The primary attraction was the concession stand.

Today, after years of experience, one rule holds true: If you can't get the people out of their cars, you can't make any money. With the cost of film rental being so high, the larger part of ticket sales goes back to the distributor of the movie. So profits generally don't come from ticket sales. It is the dollars that patrons spend inside the concession stand that owners can hold onto.

In 1952, it was estimated that for every dollar a movie ticket brought in, another 45 cents would be earned in the concession stand. However, just a few years earlier, drive-in snack bars were not much more than a counter. The same type of layout that could be found at a county fair was used. Patrons would walk up to the

Two young ushers rest at the Riverside Auto Theatre snack bar. Notice that the snack bar stand is a rather crude walk-up booth rather than a full-fledged concession stand. Ralph Bieber

An owner anticipates a busy evening as he prepares boxes of popcorn for the upcoming show. Before snack bar efficiency was realized, it was common to prepare mass quantities of food as exhibitors only had approximately 10 minutes to sell snacks during intermission. Ralph Bieber

Filmack/Mark Bialek

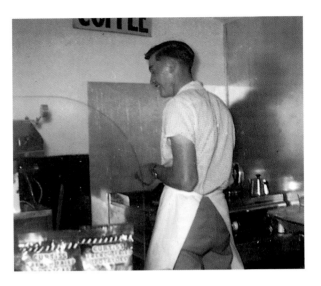

Raymond Harris prepares hamburgers and hot dogs at the Terrell Drive-In Theatre in Terrell, Texas. Raymond Harris

The local postman and another hungry patron enjoy tasty treats at the Terrell Drive-In Theatre's walk-up style snack bar. Raymond Harris

TAKE HOME BIG Profits when you take REFRESHMENTS TO THE PUBLIC with a Snack-Kar

The marketers behind the Snack-Kar claimed: "This is an opportunity for any man who realizes that refreshment stands cannot be taken to the customer, but the merchandise in a Snack-Kar can." The Snack-Kar boasted of carrying 135 10-cent drinks, 150 5-cent Cracker Jack boxes, 150 10-cent peanuts bags, 280 10-cent popcorn boxes, 365 15-cent hot dogs, and 288 10-cent ice cream bars. The cart was heated, cooled, and lighted, but proved impractical for drive-in theaters. Andy Hanson

A young vendor goes from car to car selling his goods. Two of his most popular items on cool spring nights were hot chocolate and coffee. Sales of such hot drinks were practically unheard of at traditional indoor movie houses. The Academy of Motion Picture Arts and Sciences

Donald Schafer (right), one of 40 employees working at Michael Redstone Drive-In Theatres, serves a food order to hungry young moviegoers. Carhop service was popular during the early days of drive-in theaters. UPI/Bettmann

stand, place an order, and be served without walking into a separate building. Owners would pop popcorn and cook up various foods like a family picnic. But as the years passed, owners found that large shares of their income were coming from the concession stand. And for good reason. The concession stand provided a different type of food that cost little and could be sold at a considerably marked-up price. In addition, families found they could go to the drive-in and not have to worry about dinner. They could spend the whole night outside without having to prepare a meal. It was different, too! Sodas, popcorn, french fries, hamburgers, hot dogs, corn dogs, candy bars, and cigarettes were common fare at the concession stand. Owners had finally discovered the source of their profits.

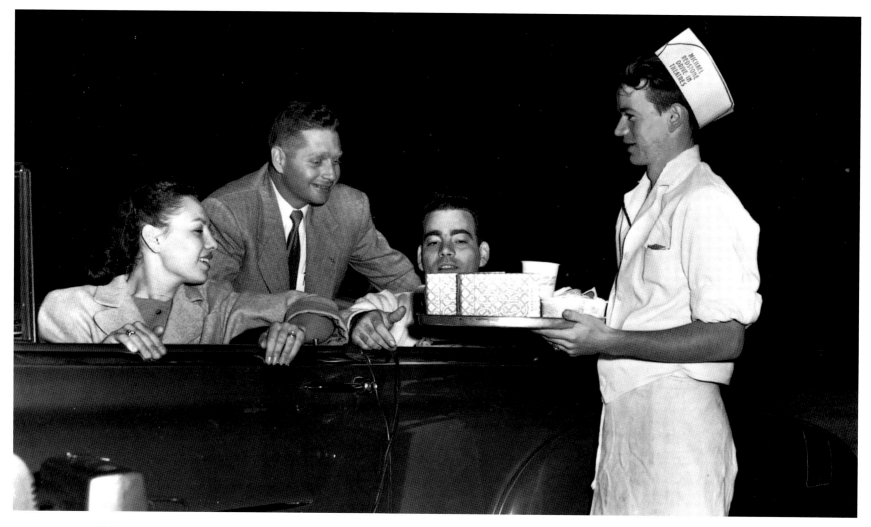

However, the concession stand had one major problem. It had only a short intermission time in which to sell concessions to the entire theater. Various remedies were tried. An early attempt was car-to-car service. "Snack-Kar's" provided a way in which vendors could go from one vehicle to another throughout the movie and sell goods. These vending carts were equipped with previously unknown facilities, such as heating, lighting, and cooling capabilities. They boasted of profits of $200 per day! And, if he so chose, the theater owner could take his concession business around town and make money outside of the theater. Recommended outlets included street vending, amusement parks, beaches, race tracks, resorts, stadiums, highways, baseball games, fireworks displays, political rallies, playgrounds, and parades. At the drive-in theaters, however, these carts had one major drawback. The moviegoers simply did not like salesmen roaming from car to car trying to turn a buck. Many felt it interfered with the movie, and others thought it to be offensive or pushy. In the end, the patrons won. The concept of the Snack-Kar, although it was a big hit early on, quickly failed, and owners looked toward other solutions.

Originally, indoor snack bars were laid out in such a fashion that customers simply crowded the counter. Unfortunately, this arrangement only created more problems, as moviegoers simply rushed the counter for fear of missing any part of the second feature. In later years, concession stands became more organized and efficient. James Tucker

The "Little Drivers Club" was located inside a drive-in concession stand in Miami, Florida. Here, kids could enjoy refreshments with their young moviegoing peers.

This menu from the Golden Spike Drive-In made ordering food easy. The menu was handed to moviegoers as they passed the theater box office. Later, when the carload got hungry, they would simply check off what items they wished to purchase, and an attendant would promptly deliver the food to the car. Michael Witzel

Architect Jack Vogel created many colorful drawings that accompanied drive-in theater proposals. In his rendering of the perfect concession stand, Vogel illustrates how people might enjoy lingering at the refreshment center if it were arranged in a more movie-friendly manner. Here, not only are tables and chairs set up, but a large picture window is provided so patrons could watch the movie. Mark Bialek

DRIVE-IN THEATRE
CONCESSION STAND
JACK K. VOGEL
REGISTERED ENGINEER

A number of happy attendants await the intermission rush. Candies are arranged so customers can help themselves, thus freeing concession employees to handle popcorn, soda, and hot food orders.
Pacific Theatres

This advertisement hyped the benefits of the Glenray hot dog cooker, which let the juices of the hot dog run from one end to the other. This type of literature was given to theater owners by companies trying to sell their various snack bar contraptions.

One answer to the Snack-Kar was window service. Here, moviegoers would simply turn on their parking lights and an attendant would come to the vehicle. The attendant would then take the order, get the food, give correct change, and go onto the next car. However, this proved to be even less efficient than a central concession stand, as theaters would have to hire extra employees to man the lot.

The talk-back system, another variation of the car-hop, was used at both the Park Drive-In of Greensboro, North Carolina, and the Cowtown Drive-In of Fort Worth, Texas. With this setup, a patron was given a detailed menu upon entering the theater. Then, when hungry, he could order through a speaker system installed next to the movie speaker. Unfortunately, this curb service variation also required extra help to run food across the huge drive-in lot. Soon, the talk-back system was dropped. Although personal and quaint, car-hop services eventually disappeared forever.

This photo and its caption are from the Motion Picture Herald, *an industry publication that was distributed to theater owners and operators.* The Academy of Motion Picture Arts and Sciences

Drive-In with Four-Section Cafeteria

The busy scene of activity above was taken in the cafeteria of the new Holiday drive-in in St. Louis, shortly after its recent opening. Refreshment operation at the 1000-car theatre is unique in many respects, including the fact that the owners, Jablonow-Komm Theatres, Inc., plan to open the cafeteria in the daytime by drawing patronage from factory workers in the adjacent area. The cafeteria is divided into four large sections, each having the same equipment to dispense the same foods and beverages, and the menu ranges from popcorn to chicken dinners. Expansive dining facilities are also provided patrons—both inside the cafeteria and in an adjoining patio. A complete description of the refreshment layout and the entire drive-in is reported in an article in the *Better Theatres* section of this issue beginning on page 18.

With concession stand profitability realized by the late-1940s, many new owners were able to incorporate concession stands into the architecture of their buildings. Such a centralized food service area soon became part of any drive-in theater layout, oftentimes built adjacent to the projection booth and rest rooms. This type of layout allowed the owner to build just one multipurpose building to serve his customers.

By the early 1950s, the concession stand was a permanent and successful drive-in fixture—and it was packed! Families would flock to the theater, and it wasn't always to see the movie. Hotel and restaurant business owner Morris Gordon noted, "It has been

proved that the title of a motion picture attraction on the marquee is sometimes of lesser importance than the offerings sold in the concession building." Going "out" to eat was a relatively new concept, and now it could be done with the added entertainment of a movie. The concession stand was a hit!

With patrons now up and making their way to the snack bar during intermission, theater owners scampered to find a way to make the walk safe. After all, many drive-ins were built on the outskirts of town where, after sundown, it gets *very* dark. To rectify the situation, owners began to install tall lights that stood over the theater's grounds. Most of these lights were affixed to telephone poles or other tall structures at the back of the parking lot. The lamps, usually fitted with a green gel to soften the effects of the illumination, were soon known as "moonglow" lights, because they supposedly resembled the light reflected off the moon. Moonglow lights were strategically located and colored so they wouldn't interrupt the presentation of the movie. Such light would fill in the shadows just enough to allow moviegoers safe jour-

neys to the restroom or snack bar.

Operator Wilfred P. Smith realized the potential of the "profiteria" and took every step he could to maximize profits. In an attempt to hurry patrons through the line even faster, Smith hypothesized, "An attendant behind the refreshment counter can hold two cups of normal size in one hand while turning the faucet to allow flow of a soft drink with the other hand. If this same attendant had a pedal attached to the dispensing unit, he could then

The Pizza Parlor— A Drive-In Invention?

Most young people can't imagine a mall without a pizza shop or a street corner without a Pizza Hut. Today, the cheesy delight can be found in grocery store freezers and restaurants across America. And although tipping the pizza delivery person has since replaced tipping the service station attendant, there was a time when pizza parlors simply did not exist—except at the drive-in theater. Remembering the best years of his theater days, Walt Thayer of Washington's United Drive-Ins commented, "People would come to get pizza and not stay for the movie. There were no pizza parlors then, and drive-ins were one of the first places you could buy a cooked pizza."

This photo from the Washington Post & Times Herald, *considered a very dignified publication in 1955, shows that the entire family can enjoy a fresh pizza at the drive-in theater.* The Academy of Motion Picture Arts and Sciences

Sales took off, and soon pizza became one of the most popular drive-in concession stand items. Today, a piping-hot pizza can still be purchased at drive-in theaters across the country. At the Kearney Drive-In in Kearney, Nebraska, the crackly recording reminds patrons that, "...if you would like to purchase a pizza, simply turn on your parking lights and one of our attendants will be right out to take your order." What better food could you want while watching a movie?

Tasty pizza, served hot and fresh, was first available at the drive-in theater. This woman serves up a pie in Valparaiso, Indiana, in 1965 at the 49er Drive-In. Bruce Shinabarger

Images like this one would flash up on the screen at intermission time. They urged customers to hurry to the snack bar for a hot pizza. Filmack/Mark Bialek

This still from one of Filmack's promotional movies shows the family at the bright and cheery concession stand. While little Ginger is delighted to have her own box of popcorn, dad orders up two hamburgers for himself and mom. Notice the prices of the other items at the concession stand, a far cry from today's $3 box of popcorn. Filmack/Mark Bialek

Many promotional films, like this one, encouraged early arrival at the theater. By doing this, theater owners could cash in on early trade by selling full dinners to families. After the kids finished, they might tire themselves on the theater's playground equipment and work up a powerful thirst. This was an excellent way to get the family back into the refreshment stand again before the movie started. Filmack/Mark Bialek

hold two cups in each hand and double his sales." The problem of too many customers in too little time had still not been solved.

To help expedite the process, restaurant and hotel equipment business owner Morris Gordon suggested that 75 percent of any theater's concession business should be done during the 10-minute break. To do so, he suggested a new kind of layout for the concession stand. "In our experience, we have discovered that the cafeteria style counter is vastly superior to the older type of front counter service. In theaters holding from 600 to 1,000 cars, the four-lane cafeteria should be installed. The four lanes should be identical, each serving the same wares, preferably with turnstiles at the beginning of each lane for protection against pilfering." This type of layout caught on fast. Old theaters were

The Drizzle Guard was an item a
theater owner could sell in the
concession stand right beside
the hot-buttered popcorn and
delicious chocolate candies.
This contraption was attached
to the front of the car and
protruded out over the
windshield; it supposedly kept
drizzle or light rain off the
window. The only weather that
would shut down a theater was
snow or fog.

These three stills from various
Filmack trailers motivated
thousands of moviegoers to buy
food. Hot dogs were always a
staple of any drive-in theater
concession stand. In fact, today,
the boiled hot dog is one food
that most theaters can still
serve. The more traditional
hamburger or french fry is now
virtually unheard of, as
insurance costs have made grills
and frying vats too costly for
most owners. Filmack/Mark
Bialek

being converted to provide such a service,
and new ones were being built with the new
concept already in place. Theater owners
were finally making more money quicker with
the notion of "self-service."

Now that the concession stand was per-
fected, it was used as a drawing card to bring
in even more customers. Special tickets were
handed out that gave away free drinks or
sandwiches. Buy-one-get-one-free coupons
were issued to bring in families that might
otherwise think costs were too high. Even
special events like dances and bands were
organized to draw moviegoers out earlier in

Dancing Hot Dogs and Countdown Clocks

For many people, the memory of an animated hot dog dancing across the screen at a drive-in theater is very vivid. And who doesn't remember the clock counting down the minutes before the next show? "You now have 4 minutes until the show starts..." Everyone scrambled about the theater—the concession boy couldn't pour fountain soda quick enough—and moviegoers loaded up on hot'n greasy snacks. Hey, it's intermission time, folks!

Chicago's Filmack Studios, which is still being run today by the founder's grandson, Robert Mack, is responsible for creating some of the most memorable intermission trailers of all time. Catering to both indoor and outdoor theater owners, the company became a well-known name in the 1950s, as it provided owners with nearly every type of promotional material they needed. Filmack movie trailers suggested moviegoers enjoy some "taste-tempting ice cream" and warned us when it was time to go "back to the show." They also told drive-in patrons not to "...drive away without first removing the in-car speaker."

After it appeared on the screen, this little hot dog would ask..."Hi! Ya hungry? Look'n for a tempting treat? Hold on 'til I absorb some heat. Some added tang might please you too. I'll slide into an oven-fresh bun, and I'm ready for your eat'n fun! Why don't you try a juicy-good hot dog? Mmmm, delicious!" Filmack/Mark Bialek

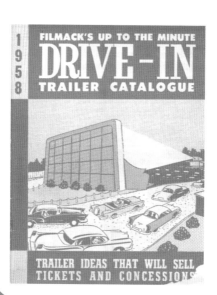

Filmack Studios mailed out trailer catalogues like this one to theater owners across the United States. The catalogues were packed full of the latest trailers and advertising suggestions available from Filmack.

Filmack would send its Drive-In Trailer Catalogue to every ozoner it knew. The catalogue was packed full of "trailer ideas that will sell tickets and concessions." The trailers reminded moviegoers that the refreshment stand offered everything from baby bottle warmers to "delicious refreshments and confections." Although the more popular trailers were simply mass-produced and sent to theaters, many of the promotional films could be specially tailored to feature one's own food or concession stand specialty.

Over the years, various companies like The Armour Company and The Alexander Film Company followed in the footsteps of Filmack Studios. And to their credit, hot dog sales soared!

A four-year-old Kipp Teague celebrates his birthday in 1960 by enjoying a game of Putt Putt before a show at Harvey's Drive-In Theatre in Lynchburg, Virginia. The massive drive-in screen looms in the background. Kipp Teague

Even television's Captain Kangaroo entices youngsters to enjoy a chocolate treat.

the evening. This practice was staged in the hopes that patrons would also enjoy dinner at the theater. Without question, promotional stunts and activities played a key role in the success of the concession stand, and ultimately the profitability of the drive-in. "If the youngsters' visit to the drive-in can be made happy and pleasant, they become excellent advertising agents whose parents are prone to indulge a request which costs so little," realized Modern Theater columnist H.F. Reves. "It has been proved that it is during this period of a child's life that he exerts the greatest influence on family spending." For this reason, theaters began to throw up playgrounds, and family patronage blossomed. Slides, swing-sets, teeter-totters, and merry-go-rounds were only the beginning. Many theaters were equipped with more exotic adventures like pony rides, train rides, and swimming pools, and even adventures for

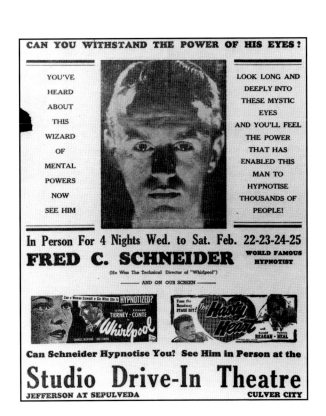

Dr. Fred C. Schneider was a classic master of the spook show. Much like the medicine wagons of the 19th century, the spook show would travel from drive-in to drive-in performing a supposedly incredible show. Billed under titles like "Chasm of Spasms," "Blood and Thunder," or "Monsters Capture Girls from Audience!" these shows were never quite what they were advertised to be. Nevertheless, performers like Fred C. Schneider, with his "masterfully hypnotic eyes," would always bring huge crowds to the theater. Security Pacific Collection, Los Angeles Public Library

85

This advertisement for Astro City, whose products were inspired by the space race, was aimed toward theater owners who wanted to improve attendance by adding a playground. Each piece of equipment was sold separately.
George Toomer

The Beverly Drive-In Theatre of Hattiesburg, Mississippi, offered miniature golf, which attracted adults as well as youngsters. Miniature golf became an integral part of drive-in entertainment by 1960 with two companies, Putt-Putt and Lomma Enterprises, building miniature golf courses for drive-ins. While Putt-Putt primarily made concrete golf courses, Lomma offered the drive-in owner the chance to add a golf course to his existing facility quite quickly. Upon sending a check for $3,900 to Lomma's Scranton, Pennsylvania, office, a golf course would be manufactured, delivered, and assembled for the theater. In fact, if the drive-in owner provided four laborers, the golf course would be up and running within 6 hours! A.J. Roquevert

adults. At Walter Reed's Woodbridge Drive-In at Woodbridge, New Jersey, elders were invited to enjoy the concrete dance floor, horseshoe pits, and shuffleboard. The Beverly Drive-In boasted a miniature golf course, which was conveniently located outside the theater lot. This type of layout allowed passing motorists to see the fun, and obviously, it was a not-too-subtle attempt to pull them into the theater. All of these attractions filled the concession stand coffers and added to the bottom line of the theater. Eventually, 43 percent of box office gross would come from concession stand sales.

The concession stand, in addition to serving refreshments, oftentimes functioned as the drive-in's "other" entertainment center. For holidays or special events, the concession stand became a stage filled with activities and contests. Halloween, for example, was a favorite night for drive-in moviegoers and theater owners. Operators would present scary acts around the concession stand or have the employees dress up in appropriate costumes. Naturally, horror films were also shown, as opposed to the regular fare. One theater, the Blue-Dell Drive-In, drew crowds by staging a fright show on top of its concession stand roof. Here, one of the moviegoers, instantly turning into a monster, would jump down and scare the other patrons. It was pure gimmick and camp, perhaps, but the stunt did attract attention. More popular than concession stand acts, however, were the contests. At

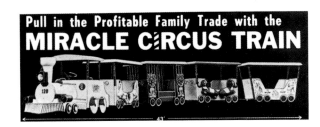

the Pacific Theatre chain of drive-ins in southern California, the concession stand was the center for contests and drawings. On one particular evening a washer and dryer would be given away; on another night, a cash jackpot would be the grand prize. Occasionally, a lucky license plate number would be drawn, or hung on the concession stand; if your license plate matched the designated number, you won a soft drink. Then there were the free passes for those who arrived barefoot, name-that-tune contests, and free admission for twins.

The concession stand has performed many functions through the years, but its primary mission of generating money remains its most important role for driven-in owners. But for patrons, it is the center of social activity, great food, and good times.

The Miracle Whirl Sales Company of Grinnell, Iowa, was a major manufacturer of drive-in playground equipment. Shown here is its most popular playground toy, which was a variation of a merry-go-round. In addition, the company constructed the Miracle Whirl, the Miracle Circus Train, and the Miracle Fairyland, which came complete with slides and swing sets. The Academy of Motion Picture Arts and Sciences

The drive-in playground, as shown here in Grayslake, Illinois, soon became an integral part of any successful theater.

The Miracle Circus Train didn't even need tracks. Trains like this could be found at many theaters across the country trying to pull in family fare. The train would usually pick up kids at a given location and then drive them around the theater lot.

The Bel-Air Drive-In in Detroit, Michigan, went all out and provided audiences with one of the best-equipped theater playgrounds in America. The 1,800-car theater was built for $400,000 and, as shown here, featured a miniature train for the kiddies.

Swimming at the drive-in! This unknown outdoor theater built a swimming pool to bring in additional patrons. The pool was a way for the theater to make money during the daytime hours. The Academy of Motion Picture Arts and Sciences

The Sioux Drive-In of Pierre, South Dakota, was unique in that the theater doubled as a sandwich shop. At this ozoner, patrons could enter and park in one of two lots. In the first, they could simply purchase a ticket and park as they would at a traditional drive-in movie theater. There, they could then purchase foods from the concession stand. At the second entrance, hungry motorists would forego the admission price, park, and purchase foods in a lot that was hidden from the screen. This allowed the facility to function as a theater and a restaurant. At the far right of the structure was a small ticket booth. Atop the sandwich shop stood the caretaker's apartment, manager's office, and projection booth.

Pony rides have always been a great way of generating business. The Gratiot Drive-In in Gratiot, Michigan, offered free pony rides to keep the kiddies happy. Pony rides and monkey villages became quite common at outdoor theaters during the 1950s.

Another step in the evolution of the in-car speaker. This Motiograph model featured a standard light and a service signal light. The service signal light could be switched on to summon an attendant, who would then bring food or drink to the patron's car during the movie. The standard light lit the area around the speaker pole. The Academy of Motion Picture Arts and Sciences

Shown as it appears today is the concession stand at Bengie's Drive-In Theatre in Baltimore, Maryland. The theater is a popular spot for many Baltimore area residents, and it continues to see a strong business. Parked out front is the owner's restored 1956 Buick Roadmaster. Lawrence R. Loy

Disneyland wasn't the only place that featured a monorail. At the Bayshore-Sunrise Drive-In Theatre, this "Mono-Rocket," manufactured by Ray Maker of Oakland, California, provided youngsters with an open-air, power-driven ride. The track was circular and measured 300 feet in length. The Academy of Motion Picture Arts and Sciences

The Rainbow Gardens Drive-In Theatre and Amusement Park near McKeesport, Pennsylvania, featured several small motor boats on a custom-built lake. The ride was an excellent drawing card for early food sales; it also increased ticket sales by as much as 30 percent. The Daily News, McKeesport, Pennsylvania

CHAPTER 4

SECOND FEATURE 1945 to 1955

While the outdoor theater business was flourishing, the audience was changing. No longer were theaters packed with families and children. Parents now had television and didn't need to leave home. But while mom and dad watched Ed Sullivan in the living room, young lovers looked desperately for some form of privacy—any privacy. According to theater owner Sam Kirkland, "parking" was illegal during the late-1950s and early 1960s. And while drive-in theaters offered the usual fare of movies and snacks, they also embraced the idol of most teens—the automobile. Thus the drive-in became the perfect place to date, and privacy was no longer an issue. It was a newly found outlet, and the kids flocked. They flocked to date and be alone, they flocked to eat corn dogs and gulp cherry sodas, they flocked to show off their new clothes, and they flocked to see schlocky movies like *I Was A Teenage Werewolf* and *The Blob*. Overnight the drive-in re-emerged as the teenager's paradise, and film studios were happy

Filmack Studios of Chicago, Illinois, produced a number of informational trailers for outdoor theaters. Shown here is a frame that addressed an all-too-common problem at drive-in theaters. Moviegoers would start up their car and take off without first removing the in-car speaker. Filmack/Mark Bialek

In the 1950s, Ford Motor Company recognized the importance of the drive-in theater's role in American society. This advertisement, showcasing Ford's new 1955 Sunliner, ran in popular magazines like Saturday Evening Post, Life, and Look. Ford Motor Company

The exciting new Sunliner, a star of Ford's Fairlane series, in Goldenrod Yellow with Raven Black.

Don't miss the DOUBLE FEATURE of the year!

Thunderbird Styling!

Trigger-Torque Power!

Picture, if you will, 16 body styles in the star-studded new Ford line. Each has a generous helping of Thunderbird styling. In a flicker, you see why so many want and buy the new Ford—for its looks! There's more than a touch of jauntiness to its slim, trim lines and flat rear deck. There's beauty—both inside and out—in the exciting, youthful color combinations. There's deep-down comfort for every relaxed inch of you, in the extra-wide seats in the roomy Luxury Lounge interior. And the extra beauty of the fabrics is this — they're as durable as they are good-looking.

The stellar attraction in the "moving" picture is Ford's exclusive Trigger-Torque power just under your toe, waiting to answer your instant power request. Answer it does—supplying you with eager response that whisks you out away from heavy traffic. It puts you ahead, when going ahead is the thing to do. It puts you ahead with a feeling of confident security. Any of Ford's three new and stout-hearted engines is ready to play this key role for you, especially when cast with the new Speed-Trigger Fordomatic. Why don't you plan to enjoy this most superb "road show" performance in years?

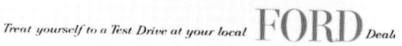

Treat yourself to a Test Drive at your local FORD Deal

Better than the movies! This young couple partakes of a little front-seat romance. In later years many drive-in theaters came to be known as "passion pits," as they were the only place teenagers could be alone. Archive Photos

to cater to them. One company that was instrumental in the production of teenage-geared movies was American International Pictures, which was co-founded by Samuel Z. Arkoff and James Nicholson. "The teenager had never counted before," quipped Arkoff. "Sure, they made movies like *Black Beauty*, but that wasn't a teenage picture, that was a picture for the little kiddies!" Suddenly, film-makers realized a previously unexploited audience. The new teenage movies didn't lecture young people, rather they were about young people, about their problems with parents, society, school, and relationships. And the movies made money—tons of money. Soon, advertisers and manufacturers began to suit the young Americans as well. Commercials for everything from jeans and hair potions to sodas and swimwear began to make their way to advertising venues on the national level. And while this new audience packed theaters, it also brought with it a stigma that

The Passion Pit

Sam Kirkland has worked at the Sky-Vue Drive-In since he was 10 years old. After the owner retired, he purchased the theater, cleaned it up, and operates the drive-in successfully today. This is his favorite story from the back row of the passion pit.

In the old days I got to the point where if I didn't see two heads and couldn't identify them both, I didn't stop and ask them if they wanted spray for mosquitoes, because it was the passion pit. Of course, the strangest thing that happened at the Sky-Vue was back when I was about 12 or 13 years old and I had never seen a naked person before; we were real protective in my family. Then one night the cars all got to honking, and at an outdoor theater when the cars start honking you know you've got a real problem. So grandma sent me over to the projection booth to check with the projectionist and see if there was anything wrong with the film. He said, "No, no there's nothing wrong with the film. Maybe they're having a fight out back!" Course, in the olden days they did have a lot of scuffles at the theater, so I went running out back to about the middle of the theater. I saw all these lights. So I went on up closer and there was a big ole' van. And on top of it there was a boy and a girl, the best I can remember in their middle twenties, and they were stark naked—and you know what they were doing on top of that van. Well, these other cars had backed out from their speaker poles and they were shining their lights up on top of this van. They were having their own show out there!

"Who me? Sure, I'm snapping beans," says this lady patron, as she and her husband sit in their car and combine business with pleasure. The drive-in theater truly was a place where you could do anything in the comfort of your own automobile. The Academy of Motion Picture Arts and Sciences

A promotional poster from the American International Pictures release I Was A Teenage Werewolf, *the first movie to have the word "teenage" in the title.*

would plague ozoners for years to come—two-bit love.

New drive-in theaters were beginning to dot the highways of America, and teens loved it! The back row had become the place for lovers in love. Even good old Barney Fife invited Juanita to the Mount Pilot Drive-In Theater on an episode of *The Andy Griffith Show.* All across the country, heads were missing, windows were fogged, and no one saw the movies anymore. Soon, the ozoner gained a new nickname—"the passion pit." The already meager family-oriented business fell drastically. Operator Herbert Ochs, who owned several drive-in theaters in the Dayton, Ohio, area remarked, "We have promoted our place as a family theater and if you watch the cars as they come out you will see that it is a family trade we are getting. We keep plenty of attendants on the lot and the cars are parked from the front in the order they enter. There is no such thing as parking in isolated spots." Regardless of Ochs' crusade to keep young love out of the theaters, his defensive remarks illustrate the fear many owners had of losing their family trade. And they did.

Children bundle up to watch a western at the Bay-Shore Sunrise Drive-In in 1955. Many patrons brought lawn chairs and blankets to watch outdoor movies. Sam Falk, New York Times Pictures

A Spectacular Color Climax

American International Pictures (AIP) had long tried various tricks and advertising campaigns to lure jaded teenagers to its movies. AIP had a reputation of being frugal. Its pictures were always made on a shoestring budget, the story was always written around a marketable title, and many of the films were shot in only 2 or 3 days. The bottom line? Get kids into the theater without spending any money!

One of the most obscure marketing techniques used by AIP was the promise of splendid color. That's right, glorious, spectacular color—and it worked. Trying to increase its box-office share, AIP tried a new advertising campaign, which boasted that a given film had a wonderful color climax. The posters were in color, and the trailers were in color. One would genuinely think he was going to see a color movie. The film would begin, and it would be in black and white—until the last sixty seconds. Then suddenly, miraculously, in a way that had nothing to do with the plot, the characters, or anything that was happening the movie jumped into color, just as promised. AIP managed to pull gullible teens into the theaters to see the new technology, but the studio only splurged to film the last sixty seconds in color, a more expensive process by its very nature.

When making such films, AIP would shoot the color finale on "re-cans," a re-spooled, unused portion of film that was left over from the shooting of a real color film. The color re-cans were cheaper as they were—and are—mostly used

I was a Teenage Frankenstein was promoted as if it were a color film. These cardboard stock posters were standard advertising materials for American International Pictures (AIP). About eight or nine of the small posters were sent to theaters to be hung in the concession stand window and promote upcoming films which, in some cases, had not even been shot. AIP employed two men who did nothing but paint posters every day. It is said that the film industry often joked, "If AIP could put sprocket holes on the posters, they'd make pretty good movies."

for camera and light tests. The gimmick was used in films like *I Was A Teenage Frankenstein*, *The Amazing Colossal Man*, and *How To Make A Monster*.

the best...any way you look at them!!!

A-1
TAPER
IVYS

 MANUFACTURING CO.

1242 Santee St., Los Angeles 15, Calif.

Taper Ivys are campus favorites because they're styled just right for comfortable fit and neat appearance... any way you look at them. Tapered legs, straight front, back strap set onto darts. Choose your color in longer wearing, high lustre twill or popular polished cotton. California styled and tailored by the originators of the famous Angeles Peggers®.

Owners quickly tried strategies that would promote the beloved family quality of the drive-in. Many theaters offered tours of the grounds, complete with free refreshments, to show youngsters and their parents what a clean and wholesome place the drive-in was. Operators tried to illustrate their good intentions to their audience. "We wish Walt Disney could make a picture a week or a day—so that we could always give you a clean, amusing Disney picture. But unfortunately that isn't possible, so we do our utmost to give you the best, most wholesome pictures from all sources that can be had," explained Pacific Theaters executive Robert Selig. "We wanted you to come and see us in the daytime, which is something that few people have occasion to do, so that you can balance the facts that you have seen against the unfounded derogatory rumors you sometimes hear from critics."

Other owners opened their arms to the

By 1955, some theater owners were becoming concerned about the rising popularity of television. The 87 Drive-In owner obviously had that in mind when he designed his theater to look like the back of a huge television. When this particular owner opened his theater, he hired an airplane to fly over the town and drop leaflets announcing the grand opening. Many of the leaflets contained free passes to the theater!

A group of youngsters and their parents proudly pose for a publicity photo after a round of soap-box derby races at the Drive-In Theater in Terre Haute, Indiana. Notice the marquee in the background. At many theaters, Mondays and Wednesdays were often billed as "buck night." On such an evening, an entire car load would be admitted for a single dollar. Indiana Historical Society

More companies were beginning to use the drive-in as a backdrop for selling their products. This advertisement from A-1 Manufacturing Company shows just how cool teens can be if they wear slick, new Taper Ivys jeans to the drive-in. Jim Heimann

O. Winston Link's
Hotshot Eastbound

In the late-1950s, photographer O. Winston Link set out on an expedition to photograph the last of the great steam trains. Realizing that most of these trains were located in the coal fields of West Virginia and Virginia, Link began the travels that would later yield over 200 images of steam trains. Oftentimes, these photographs included people to tell a story. Most of the time nothing was staged; every photo was shot with the people going about their daily life. A typical image might portray a steam train behind two people on a park bench, or a steam train outside the window of a young couple's living room. Of all his portraits, however, Link's most famous photograph would be taken at a drive-in theater.

On August 2, 1956, Link positioned his son and his son's girlfriend in the front of a Buick convertible, which was parked at a quiet drive-in. He then arranged a series of flashes, each set to go off on an exact command, along the railroad track. Link's assistant stood behind the screen shouting, "The train is 200 feet from the screen! The train is 100 feet from the screen!" Finally, when the train was in just the right place, the shutter was opened and the flashes were fired. However, when the flashes ignited, they washed out the image on the drive-in screen, which was showing the film *Battle Taxi*. It has been rumored that Link used the frame of an earlier photograph to patch the image, but no one can be sure, as the negative is not available for inspection. The photograph, which is titled *Hotshot Eastbound*, combines the three most important modes of transportation: the plane, the train, and the automobile.

It was a hot night on August 2, 1956, as O. Winston Link made the exposures for what became his best known photograph. In the small towns of the West Virginia coal country, long trains of coal and mixed freight were commonplace, and the patrons of the Laeger Drive-In hardly even noticed this high-speed freight thundering by as they watched Battle Taxi, *a story of an air rescue team in the Korean War, starring Sterling Hayden.*
© O. Winston Link

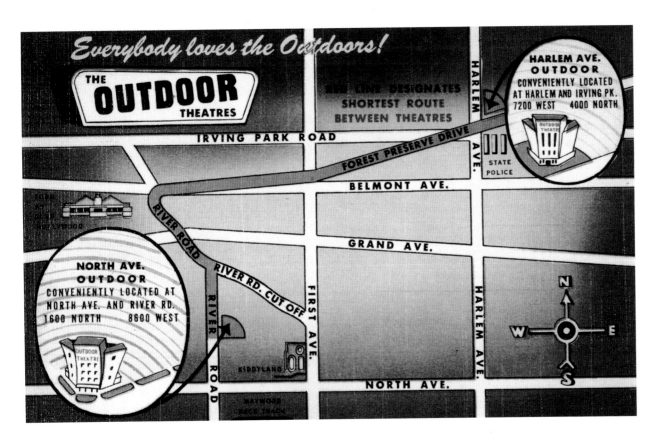

Operators frequently mailed out postcards like this one to help increase the dwindling family crowd. Lake County (Illinois) Museum, Curt Teich Postcard Archives

theaters, the drive-in continued to be the domain of teenagers during the 1960s. It was obvious to many operators that the heyday of the family drive-in theater was gone. If a theater was to remain profitable, it needed the kids and their discretionary income.

The Ozoner Overseas

All types of Americana, including drive-ins, migrated overseas. Elwood Blues best captured the global attitude in his *Made in America* album, "As you look around this round world, you go to Europe, Scandinavia, or France — everybody is doing flips and twists just to get into a genuine pair of American blue jeans. And to think we've got it all here, in America, the land of the Chrysler 440 cubic-inch engine!" Just like blue jeans and Coca-Cola, drive-ins started to catch on overseas. The first drive-in in Europe was located in Rome, Italy, and was simply called, Drive-In Cine. Built in the mid-1950s for an estimated $1.5 million, the theater held about 750 automobiles and 250 scooters.

churches, allowing them to hold outdoor services on Sunday morning. This not only helped project the wholesome outdoor image of the ozoner, but helped acquire dollars charged for rent of the facilities. However, if a church group could not afford the "suggested" rent, the theater grounds would be donated out of the good will of the drive-in, its little way of giving something back to the community.

Unfortunately, even with all these attempts to bring families back to outdoor

For a while, overseas drive-ins were packed with small European cars. However, such automobiles didn't make the moviegoing experience terribly comfortable. As a result, foreign moviegoers never did cozy up to the rather American idea of watching a movie from one's car. This drive-in in Rome, Italy, accommodated 750 cars and featured a grandstand for walk-in patrons. UPI/Bettmann

Other European ozoners followed. Many drive-ins were quickly built in Germany, a country that embraced outdoor theaters for many years. Even in the late-1980s, most of the top-grossing German screens were drive-in theaters. However, outside of Germany, overall foreign growth was difficult, and drive-in theaters saw slow progress abroad. One reason lay within the design of the European car. Remember, the American automobile was being built bigger all the time. Function was not the important part, fashion and comfort were. Europeans, who owned smaller cars, were simply not all that excited about the notion of going out to sit in one's car. Records indicate that by 1967, years after the Rome drive-in was constructed, only four drive-ins existed in Europe: Rome, Madrid, Stockholm, and Toulon in France.

Central America, like Europe, also caught drive-in fever during the 1950s. In Mexico, President Miguel Aleman showed up to cut the ribbon at the nation's first drive-in theater in 1950, the Auto Cinema Lomas in Mexico City. In 1958, Andre Lopez Salas opened the International Drive-In Theater in Bayaman, Puerto Rico. The establishment prided itself in having the newest motion picture technology—Cinemascope.

With American films playing at drive-ins around the world in the 1960s, the western quickly became a favorite among teenagers across the globe. At this drive-in located in France, teenagers not only watch an American film, but they also enjoy the experience from a great piece of Detroit iron—a Buick convertible. Archive Photos

A fancy neon sign boasts of beauty and excitement. This was the owner's subtle way of encouraging otherwise timid audiences to stop at the Victory Drive-In Theatre, which was located in Menomonee Falls, Wisconsin. Steve Fitch

The Largest Television Screen Was at a Drive-In Theater

It was September of 1952, and the Marciano-Walcott heavyweight boxing title bout was about to take place. It was going to be huge. Before the days of satellite television or HBO, independent indoor theaters would occasionally book programming, such as sporting events, on a closed-circuit basis called "theater TV." With the Marciano-Walcott fight, there was a complete television/radio blackout during the broadcast so that theaters equipped with theater TV had a complete exclusive.

Realizing that previous experiments in theater TV generally sold out in advance, the Smith Management Company decided to try something new. Rather than show the fight at one of its traditional indoor theaters that was equipped with theater TV, SMC decided to present the fight at its largest theater, where it could sell more tickets. That theater was the S-3 Drive-In in Rutherford, New Jersey.

Because the S-3 Drive-In was located in close proximity to the Philadelphia fight, the closed-circuit feed could work without problems. The owners sunk big dollars into the rental of a new projection technology that had been developed by RCA. This contraption came in the back of a semi truck, was set up in the center of the theater, and projected the broadcast onto the drive-in screen. Wooden chairs were

The RCA Instantaneous Theater TV equipment was cutting-edge technology in 1952. When it was used at the S-3 Drive-In, the huge system was mounted aboard the back of a truck, which acted as the outdoor projection booth. After the theater was packed to its 1,200-car capacity, it was estimated that no fewer than 5,000 people were turned away at the gate. At the time, the televised fight was the largest TV picture ever shown, with the longest projection throw ever used in a theater television.

set up so walk-in customers could come as well. Admission was set at $10 for a car load or $2.50 for an individual walk-in customer. By the end of the fight, the Smith Management Company estimated that it grossed approximately $16,000. It also made history by effectively creating the world's largest television screen. Ironically, it was in a drive-in theater.

While Japan might have had a great desire to build ozoners, such theaters took up far too much space. The concept of the drive-in theater was simply not feasible in a country where land was and still is so incredibly valuable. With this in mind, a company by the name of Shockiku-Fuji, which produced and distributed Japanese films, made an attempt to create a drive-in. Its method of drive-in construction and operation was innovative and practical. Using shopping mall parking lots, which were closed in the evenings, large trucks would bring in portable screens and projection equipment. Sound would then be broadcast via car radios to the theater's patrons. When the show was over, the theater would be struck and mall operations would continue the next day as if nothing happened. Box-office profits were split between the theater's proprietor and the mall. While such an idea might have been a noble attempt, the idea simply did not stick with the Japanese people.

For a while, drive-ins even became popular in Australia. There, Loews Theaters owned and operated two ozoners in 1957: a 1,000-car drive-in in Perth and a 1,400-car, two-screen complex in Sydney. But, again, the craze never caught on quite as it did in America.

The only country outside of the United States where ozoners had a strong impact was Canada, which is ironically known for its bitter-cold winter conditions. But the Canadians caught the drive-in bug and fostered some 300 outdoor theaters over the years. The first was the Skyway, which opened on July 10, 1946 near Stony Creek, Ontario. Perhaps the smallest drive-in was the 20-car screen at Loon Lake, Saskatchewan. And then there was Quebec, which, until 1967, outlawed drive-in theaters because they were viewed as passion pits. At the time, the

The Daytona Beach Drive-In Christian Church was located on South Atlantic Avenue, just between the Atlantic Ocean and the inland waterway. Services at the theater were held at 8:30 and 10:00 in the morning. Of course, Sunday School for the youngsters took place between the two services. The church, which was led by Minister Wallace Pomplun, was a worship place for people of all faiths. Brian Butko

As advertising budgets got smaller, theater owners stopped hiring professional designers and artists and began to decorate their own theaters. The Blue Moon Drive-In of St. Johnsbury, Vermont, shows the owner's attempt to tie the theater to the iconography of the surrounding land.

Roman Catholic Church, which had a significant amount of power, was able to lobby against potential builders and prevent the construction of any drive-in theaters. Nevertheless, as late as 1988, Canadian drive-in screens took in well over $4 million, an impressive figure for a rather small population base.

The Slow Descent

By the mid-1960s, the American drive-in business had fallen off and operators were making attempts to increase ticket sales. In some situations, outdoor theaters tried to improve their image by putting up new signs or painting fresh logos on their screen towers. Once again, a few operators turned to elaborate neon artwork to bring their theaters to life. As early as 1958, concerns were being raised about the outdoor theater industry reaching its saturation point. There were too many theaters being built too fast. It was difficult for small-time operators to invest large sums of money to recreate an existing drive-in facade. The 1960s saw not only a dwindling audience, but the last of the newly constructed drive-ins as well.

Business was stagnant. The theaters that were doing well were those in Alaska, where winter nighttime darkness lasted for 18 hours. In Anchorage, theater owners would run 6 or 7 movies back to back—and people showed up.

But where night wasn't so long or cold, operators had an entirely different logistical problem—daylight saving time. Although daylight saving time wasn't nationally incorpo-

Humble, yet inviting in its own way, this entryway is typical of the construction that took place during the mid-1960s. As attendance fell off, it was simply not practical to invest large amounts of capital into drive-ins.

Beneath their Cessna 120, Mr. and Mrs. Myron Leraan and Ronnie, age 4, are ready to watch **Hootenanny Hoot,** *plus two cartoons, after flying in from Northwood, Iowa. In the late 1950s, several drive-ins in New Jersey, Massachusetts, Ohio, and Iowa were equipped with runways.* Cleveland Public Library Photograph Collection

This Jack Vogel rendering of the Crockette Drive-In Theatre, which was never built, illustrates how opulent theaters could become. Sensational colors, neon artwork, and dreamy screen tower design were all combined with manicured lawns and shrubs to portray the drive-in as a fantasy land. Mark Bialek

CROCKETTE DRIVE-IN THEATRE
EAST LIVERPOOL, O.
JACK K. VOGEL
REGISTERED ENGINEER,

The Orange Drive-In and the Rise of Robert Schuller

Dr. Robert Schuller preaches from the top of the Orange Drive-In's concession stand. The theater, which was located in Garden Grove, California, was known as the world's first walk-in/drive-in church. Crystal Cathedral Ministries

It was the winter of 1955 when Robert Schuller left Chicago and headed for Garden Grove, California. His goal was to start a new ministry. Unfortunately, he literally had no place to hold services. Brainstorming locations to rent, Schuller created a list of ten ideal sites to hold a church service. They were as follows:

1. School building
2. Mortuary chapel
3. Masonic temple
4. Elks hall
5. Seventh Day Adventist Church
6. Jewish synagogue
7. Community club building
8. An acre of ground and pitch a tent
9. Drive-in theater
10. Empty warehouse

When Schuller tried to nail down a location, the list quickly dwindled. The Baptists had already rented the mortuary chapel, a community center could not be found, and it was against California state law to rent government-owned property for religious proposes. With few other options, Schuller humbly turned to the Orange Drive-In, a nearby ozoner. After securing the location for $10 per day, Schuller went door to door asking hundreds of people to come to the Sunday service. He was, to say the least, ambitious. Schuller hauled the organ from home and preached from the top of the snack bar, but that first weekend only brought 46 cars to the 1,700-car theater. It wasn't until author Norman Vincent Peale (*The Power of Positive Thinking*) later agreed to guest speak that the church took off. Humorously, the Sunday morning Peale spoke, the drive-in marquee read "Norman Vincent Peale," and underneath Peale's name in red letters it said "To Hell and Back." Someone had forgotten to take

Shown here is Dr. Robert Schuller (left) with guest speaker Norman Vincent Peale at the Orange Drive-In Theatre in 1957. Crystal Cathedral Ministries

down the name of the previous night's movie during all the excitement. Perhaps it was because of the marquee mix-up, or maybe it was just good publicity on Schuller's behalf, but for some reason people turned out in droves that Sunday morning. Over 4,000 people showed up to hear Norman Vincent Peale. The rest is history. Schuller's church has served as a model for drive-in churches around the country. By 1960, there were over 75 such churches. At some, grapefruit juice and wafers were passed from car to car for communion services. Schuller's ministry continued to operate out of the Orange Drive-In for some six years. Today, Schullers' ministry is internationally televised each week and reaches over 30 million viewers.

Many theater owners allowed Sunday church services to take place at their drive-ins. Churchgoers would listen to the sermon over the in-car speaker system and watch the minister preach from on top of the snack bar. These outdoor services offered churchgoers the same conveniences as moviegoers and helped the theaters improve their image within the community. Here, the Orange Drive-In hosts a service led by Dr. Robert Schuller. Crystal Cathedral Ministries

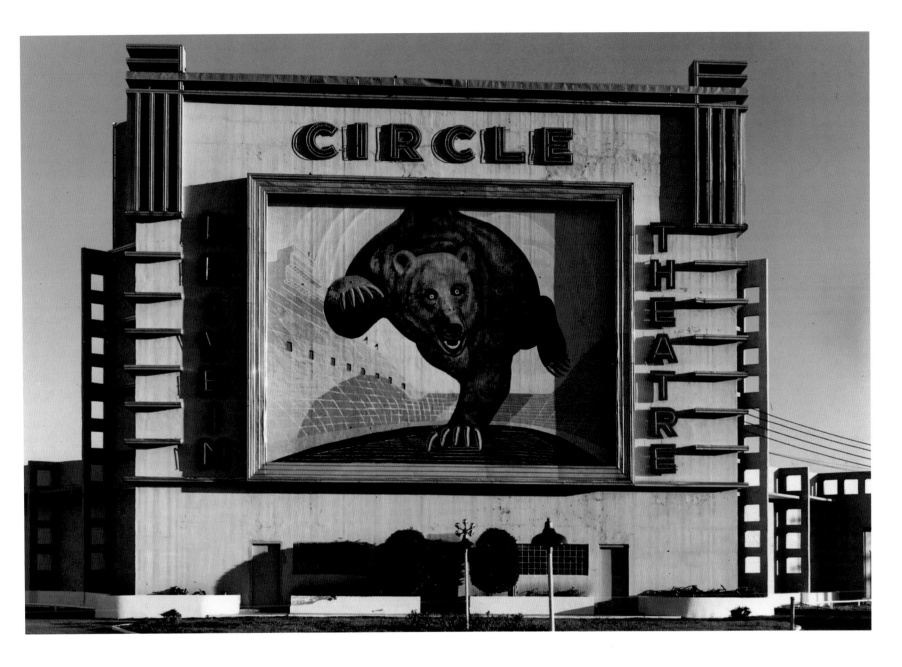

rated in the United States until 1967, it had been a problem for some drive-ins as early as 1949. With the practice becoming more and more common, theater owners had to start already-late show times even later. And while, in some cases, the later show times increased pre-movie concession sales, the overall effects were discouraging.

These late starts had such an impact that the Theater Owners of America (TOA) made a legitimate effort to create a daylight drive-in screen. Such a screen would supposedly improve picture quality and allow owners to start the show times, at the very least, during dusk. The National Association of Theater Owners (NATO) even put together a committee, the Drive-In Technical Committee, that oversaw the pioneering of this new brainchild. Such a screen was to be developed using hundreds of tiny mirrors that would enhance the picture quality, but its creators couldn't find a way to overcome the ambient light from the sun—it was simply too powerful. Consequently, daylight projection was quietly dropped.

The Circle Drive-In circa 1964. During the heyday of the drive-in, many owners hired artists and neon glass workers to design the otherwise empty side of the screen tower. When the Circle was originally built in 1947, the theater sported an Indian-themed mural. When the painting became worn, it was replaced with a bear, the mascot of the local college, Baylor University. Windy Drum 1964, from the James Jasek collection

This illustration depicts the type of grand entrances architect Jack Vogel had envisioned for future drive-in construction. Classic elements include plenty of bright lights, sharp lines, and vivid colors. Mark Bialek

TICKET OFFICE · ENTRANCE

JACK K. VOGEL
ARCHITECTURAL ENGINEER

In the 1970s, most owners turned to more practical methods of theater decoration. Here, the Razorback Twin of Little Rock, Arkansas, is covered with a weatherproof siding and decorated very simply. The owner did splurge, however, by including a mural. Like the Circle Drive-In, the Razorback Twin sports a college mascot, the University of Arkansas razorback. Steve Fitch

The Tri-City Drive-In featured a highly detailed mural on its screen tower. Unfortunately, rising maintenance costs and diminishing attendance forced the Tri-City to make only necessary building repairs. Thus, the mural was left to deteriorate.

The late 1960s witnessed very poor drive-in business. The greasy-haired teens went off to college, and once again, the drive-in was left looking for an audience. Family fare simply would not play, the teen audience had all but disappeared, and first-run features were still difficult to obtain. Many theaters turned to R-rated pictures and limited show times to weekends. Economics came into play and anything that could cut the cost of operation was attempted. As a result, many theaters were not maintained properly. Snack bars and restrooms began to show their age. Speakers began to fail from old and weathered wiring. Screens went unpainted, and parking lots were not resurfaced when they should have been. Viewing a movie became a chore.

Construction of new theaters came to an abrupt halt. Architect Jack Vogel continued to design new theaters with futuristic facades and grand entryways, but most were not built as financing fell through. Huge pieces of property were being developed into housing developments or retail outlets; the drive-ins just couldn't compete as revenue generators. Investors began to question the financial viability of the ozoner.

Existing theaters tried to pep up their grounds by appealing to the local color. Operators created simple murals and paintings that were intended to draw the same crowd as earlier murals, but they did not work. Funds were short, and owners would do most of the artwork themselves, giving the theater plenty of character, but in the process eliminating any remnants of showmanship.

The great theaters had all been built. They had seen their days of long lines at the ticket booths, packed lots and refreshment stands, and playgrounds full of kids. They didn't have to worry about newer, more grandiose theaters being built to compete with them, for they never came. Rather, the old theaters limped along, waiting for a second chance.

Elvis Presley and the Drive-In Theater

Just outside Amarillo, Texas, the Tascosa Drive-In entryway stretches through the sky. Unfortunately, its days of progressive operation have long since passed.

Elvis Presley loved to go to the movies. But with fame came a price, the loss of anonymity. As one might assume, it was always difficult for Elvis and his friends to attend movies without causing a huge scene. As a result, he would frequently rent an entire indoor theater and sponsor a private screening of a movie for family and friends. But this became an exercise in planning and coordinating, and it left no room for spontaneity. His solution? The

The Bellevue Drive-In in Memphis, Tennessee, was only a short distance from Elvis Presley's Graceland. The theater was located on Bellevue Drive, a street which later became Elvis Presley Boulevard. It is assumed that this is the drive-in theater where Elvis spent his last night at home before shipping off to defend his country.

drive-in theater. In 1958 there were six drive-in theaters in Memphis, Tennessee, all of which provided Elvis and his gang a place to hang out in the privacy of their own car. According to Peter Guralnick, author of the biography *Last Train to Memphis*, the night before Elvis reported to Army service was a memorable one. "On his last night of freedom he was up all night with his friends. He and Anita and some of the boys went to the drive-in to see Tommy Sands in *Sing, Boy, Sing*, the story of the rise and fall of a rock 'n roll star told in somewhat harder-hitting terms than any of Elvis' movies. 'We pulled in to the drive-in in the Cadillac limousine,' said George Klein, 'It was kind of cold, and we all wanted to stay up with him until the last minute, you know, and keep his mind occupied so he wouldn't have to think about leaving the next day...He hadn't eaten or slept when dawn came up. "Overnight," he said, "it was all gone. It was like a dream."

That 'drive-in' that George Klein speaks about was most likely the Bellevue Drive-In on North Bellevue Boulevard. The theater was quite close to Graceland and would have been a convenient hangout for Elvis and his friends. Who says the drive-in is only for the working-class man? It was good enough for our King.

Pacific Theatres Corporation— The Finest in Outdoor Entertainment.

Pacific Theatres Corporation has long been a stronghold in the drive-in theater business. Dating back as early as the 1930s, Pacific has owned and operated theaters in the southwest part of the United States with great success. The company, which is based in Los Angeles, California, got into the outdoor theater business when the Olympic Drive-In opened in Los Angeles. The theater, which was previously known as the Pico Drive-In, was moved, intact, to its new site on Olympic Boulevard.

At one time, the Pacific Theatres Corporation of Los Angeles, California, operated over 110 outdoor theaters. Today, only four remain open in the greater Los Angeles area. Shown here is the Pacific Drive-In Theatre logo, circa 1950. Pacific Theatres

The Sunnyside Drive-In was one of many theaters built by California's Pacific Theatres Corporation. As part of the promotion for such a theater, the management offered free tours to families, schools, or companies. Groups would see the theater lot, the projection facilities, and occasionally sample concession stand foods. By doing this, owners established a friendly relationship with communities and combated the negative publicity that sometimes surrounded the drive-in theater. The Academy of Motion Picture Arts and Sciences

The neon structure at the Sunnyside Drive-In was the largest neon sign ever built for a drive-in. This theater owner followed the practices of his fellow operators and used neon to increase ticket sales from impulse patrons.

Over the years, Pacific continued to recognize the potential of drive-ins. At one point, the company operated over 100 outdoor movie theaters, most of which sported elaborate murals or paintings on their backside.

In 1964, Pacific began to interact with its neighborhood patrons. Community members could show up and take a free guided tour through the facilities, enjoy refreshments at the snack bar, and get a better idea of how the theater operated. Such activities promoted the theater, but they also developed a relationship between the theater and the surrounding community. Even during the 1964 riots in Los Angeles, a time of great civil unrest, Pacific kept its drive-ins open to the community. The company has always remained very devoted to its local patrons.

Unfortunately, in recent years, land values have made theater ownership rather impractical. In most areas of greater Los

Shown during its construction outside of Fresno, California, is one of the last great drive-in theaters ever built. After the summer of 1965, construction of outdoor theaters fell dramatically. Unfortunately, such great growth has not been seen since. The Academy of Motion Picture Arts and Sciences

Angeles, real estate values are simply too high to operate a theater that can only generate revenue at night. In fact, that first drive-in, the Olympic, was sold for 3 million dollars. It was prime real estate.

Over the years, various theater chains have done quite well by promoting and operating outdoor theaters. Gulf States operated theaters in the South, while Redstone Theaters operated in the Northeast. Rowley United maintained the south central states. In a business that is dominated by the independent, Pacific Theatres has been a corporation that has kept drive-in theaters alive in the city of Angels. Today, Pacific continues to operate four ozoners in the Los Angeles basin.

The handsome marquee of the 309 Drive-In Theatre boasted of comfortable, year-round entertainment. Archive Photos

CHAPTER 5

MONSTERS AND MAYHEM 1965 TO 1985

By the mid-1960s, teen exploitation films had hit their peak. Both ozoners and indoor theaters were littered with films like *Beach Blanket Bingo*, *It Conquered the World*, *I Was a Teenage Frankenstein*, and many others. Most of these films were produced by Samuel Z. Arkoff's American International Pictures (AIP), which put out low-budget, drive-in fare. While it was common for AIP to put together a movie or show surrounding one monster or a single big scene, most of the movies were based on the title. If someone came up with a title that sounded commercially viable yet different, the movie would be made. Such was the case with films like *The Beast with a Million Eyes*. In fact, while AIP shot *The Beast*, director Roger Corman didn't have any money to create a monster, so he didn't show one. It wasn't until after production of the movie wrapped that AIP went back in and picked up a couple of "beast shots" that could be inserted into the movie. It turned out that the monster ended up being many beams of light shining through a tin can with holes. Hundreds of pictures like this were produced over the years, many of which Corman directed.

Muscle Beach Party *epitomized the bikini movies of the early-1960s and led the way for an entire decade of exploitation films. Drive-in theaters thrived for years on such movies.*

Having always been outside the studio system, Roger Corman became infamous for his ability to bring a picture in under budget. His first film, *Monsters from the Ocean Floor*, was produced for an unprecedented budget of $18,000 in 1953. His films of the 1950s soon became testament to the theory that movies need not cost a fortune to be entertaining. Most of the 225 films Corman produced were quite successful. In fact, his box-office hits alone virtually built American International Pictures. His method was to keep films cheap and packed full of exploitation value. "Roger just told me, 'Read the script, rewrite as much as you want, but remember, Marty, that you must have some nudity at least every fifteen pages'" recalls director and past Corman employee Martin Scorsese. "'Not complete nudity, maybe a little off-the-shoulder, or some leg, just to keep the audi-

It's the game that separates the girls and the boys...into groups of two!

AMERICAN INTERNATIONAL presents

BEACH BLANKET BINGO

PATHECOLOR and PANAVISION

The BEACH PARTY gang goes SKY DIVING!

starring

FRANKIE AVALON · ANNETTE FUNICELLO · DEBORAH WALLEY · HARVEY LEMBECK

JOHN ASHLEY · JODY McCREA · DONNA LOREN | 1st RUN DALLAS!

ARAPAHO RD.	BIG D	BRUTON RD.	BUCKNER BLVD.
CHALK HILL	CREST	DENTON RD.	GARLAND RD.
GEMINI TWIN	GRANADA	HAMPTON RD.	LONE STAR
VOGUE	CINEMA BIG TOWN		IRVING IN IRVING
PLAZA IN CARROLLTON	SEE DIRECTORY ADS FOR 2ND FEATURES!		

★ **PERSONAL APPEARANCES TONITE** ★
FRANKIE AVALON AND DEBORAH WALLEY
and the CHESSMAN COMBO direct from "SHINDIG"
GEMINI TWIN, 6 P.M. ● VOGUE, 8 P.M. ● BUCKNER, 9 P.M.

Even into the mid-1960s a special guest appearance from a Hollywood star could guarantee a sold-out theater. Such was the case for the Gemini Twin Drive-In Theatre in Dallas, Texas. As promised in this advertisement, Frankie Avalon and Deborah Walley made personal appearances at the opening night of Beach Blanket Bingo. *Dallas Public Library*

ence interest up.' This was very important for the exploitation market, so it was what he had to have." Scorsese goes on to explain, "Roger had all these little ideas about how films should be made. For example, in the sound mixing, he said, 'Remember, you're mixing the entire film in three days: nine reels, three days. The first reel has to be good because people coming to the drive-in have to hear what's going on. Forget the rest of the film until you get to the last reel, because they just want to know how it turned out.'

It Conquered the World was among a number of schlocky monster movies that were drummed up for the new teenage audience.

Look out! Big rubber monsters and bad acting continued to grace the screens of ozoners across America right up until the late 1960s. This scene is from It Conquered the World.

And he said it with a straight face."

Corman's films were always geared toward the drive-in crowd, but it wasn't long before movie audiences got tired of such stories. It was then that the movies turned to pure schlock. Many titles that graced outdoor screens included *Sorority Girl*, *Motorcycle Gang*, *One Million Years B.C.*, *It's a Bikini World*, *T-Bird Gang*, and numerous other cinematic works of mediocrity. These movies had no real social or moral points. Rather, their purpose was to fill screen time and make money. Plain and simple, they were product.

Some people say that it was because studios quit making good pictures, and there are those who claim that families had other places to go and be together, but for some reason in

the late 1960s, people quit going to the drive-in movies. Attendance dropped sharply. And while a new drive-in would occasionally open featuring Cinemascope or Todd-A-O sound, the occurrence was rare. For the most part, only lonely nights lay ahead for the drive-in theater.

The Struggle to Survive

Various theaters tried to adapt to keep alive. Once again they tried to find something different that would bring in customers. The days of drive-ins being the "informal" theater were now gone. Even at indoor theaters people were beginning to feel more comfortable in a simple T-shirt and shorts, something that was relatively unheard of in earlier days.

This advertisement from the Barco Drive-In in Lamar, Missouri, is loaded with 1960s exploitation films. 20th Century-Fox got into the action with Raquel Welch's One Million Years B.C.; It's A Bikini World *promised "bikini bunnies" to be "bustin' out" all over the screen; and Roy Orbison was "America's hottest singing star." It did not matter if there was a story (or in some cases even a pretty girl), just as long as the star or title would bring people out to the movie. A.J. Roquevert*

Gala Opening Friday, April 5th
BARCO DRIVE-IN
THEATRE • LAMAR, MO.

BIG OPENING PROGRAM
Friday & Saturday
APRIL 5 & 6
TWO COLOR FEATURES!

●

OPENING NITE SPECIAL
DRIVER of CAR FREE
(FRIDAY NIGHT ONLY)

●

SAME PRICES

ALL CHILDREN
(Regardless Of Age)
ADMITTED FREE
With Both Parents!

●

Show Starts At 7:30

PRE-HISTORIC MONSTERS ROAM THE EARTH!
SEE!.... THE SALVAGE TRICERATOPS!
SEE!.... The Flesh - Eating ALLOSAURUS!
SEE!.... The Mammoth BRONTOSAURUS!
SEE!.... Monsters In Combat!

First there was man... woman...and beast... THIS IS THE WAY IT WAS
Starring RAQUEL WELCH
ONE MILLION YEARS B.C.
IN COLOR

PLUS COUNTRY MUSIC & ACTION!

AS A SINGING, SHOOTING, SON OF A GUN!
ROY ORBISON
The FASTEST GUITAR ALIVE
America's hottest singing star on the screen at last!
METROCOLOR

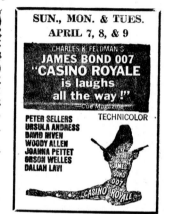

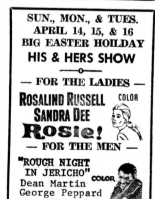

IT'S HAPPY DRIVE - IN MOVIE TIME!

122

In Monte Vista, Colorado, theater owner George Kelloff came up with a concept that kept his theater alive during those difficult times. Today, he continues to run a successful business. George built the Starlite Drive-In Theatre as a normal ozoner and operated it until business began to slow in the mid 1960s. Then, in 1964, he added a motel, converting his theater into the Best Western Movie Manor. "The Movie Manor is a movie motel," explains George Kelloff. "It's the only one of its kind because we own a drive-in theater and have motion pictures that can be seen from your unit. We have an agreement with the motion picture people to where we pay for people to stay in the motel (that way they profit, too) and yet we give a service to people who want something different. This is different. You can go to a downtown theater or a drive-in, but you can't go to a motel-drive-in."

The 66 Park In Theatre, shown here in 1992, once entertained thousands of travelers on their way to the land of milk and honey. One man who made a habit of visiting the 66 Park In is Paul Taylor, now the publisher of **Route 66** magazine. Taylor vividly recalls skipping school and taking day trips to the 66 Park In Theatre, which provided a bigger screen and better movies than his hometown drive-in. Along the way, Taylor and his friends would pick up watermelons; once there, they would have a feast while watching the movie. When the movies were over and the watermelon was gone, the youngsters would drive back home and sneak into bed— around two or three in the morning.

A lonely night at the 8th Street Drive-In Theatre in Colorado Springs, Colorado. Steve Fitch

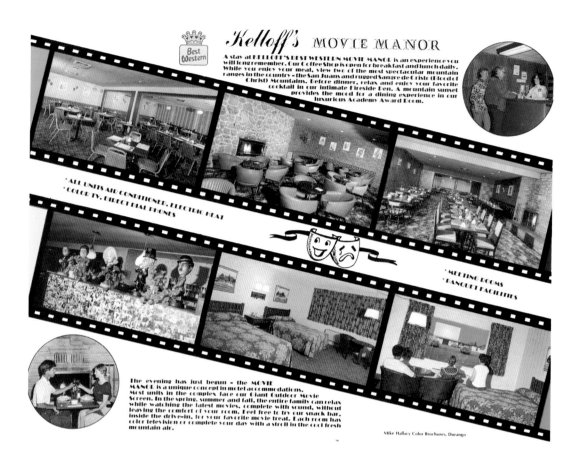

Kelloff's MOVIE MANOR

A stay at KELLOFF'S BEST WESTERN MOVIE MANOR is an experience you will long remember. Our Coffee Shop is open for breakfast and lunch daily. While you enjoy your meal, view two of the most spectacular mountain ranges in the country – the San Juans and rugged Sangre de Cristo (Blood of Christ) Mountains. Before dinner, relax and enjoy your favorite cocktail in our intimate Fireside Den. A mountain sunset provides the mood for a dining experience in our luxurious Academy Award Room.

*ALL UNITS AIR CONDITIONED, ELECTRIC HEAT
*COLOR TV, DIRECT DIAL PHONES

*MEETING ROOMS
*BANQUET FACILITIES

The evening has just begun – the MOVIE MANOR is a unique concept in motel accommodations. Most units in the complex face our Giant Outdoor Movie Screen. In the spring, summer and fall, the entire family can relax while watching the latest movies, complete with sound, without leaving the comfort of your room. Feel free to try our snack bar, inside the drive-in, for your favorite movie treat. Each room has color television or complete your day with a stroll in the cool fresh mountain air.

Mike Hallacy Color Brochures, Durango

At George Kelloff's Movie Manor, which functions as a "movie motel," patrons can lie in bed and enjoy a film from the comfort of their own room. Large picture windows allow travelers to watch the film as it shows on the nearby drive-in movie screen. Jon Bokenkamp

The drive-in in Longview, Washington, offered both AM radio and in-car speaker sound. Today, nearly all drive-in theaters offer radio sound in addition to traditional in-car speakers.

Each patron can actually watch the movie through a large picture window, and sound is individually piped into each room through a small speaker.

The Movie Manor also features a movie-themed restaurant and lounge, a private airport with two runways, snowmobiling on the Manor property, a playground, RV hookups, and a snack bar with all your favorite treats. To maintain the grounds, George and his wife Judy live at the drive-in. He explains, "We lived and still live in the middle of the drive-in theater. The wife and I built a little apartment there, right next to the projection booth and the snack bar, and we went ahead and had a living room that faced the screen."

However, most theater owners were not able to survive by creating such movie-themed resorts; they simply lacked the budget to make such modifications. Rather, a more common adaptation, especially in California, was the swap meet. Here, a section of

a theater lot could be rented for a nominal price. Many theaters simply leased the entire lot for $150 per day; this way the renter could oversee the operations of the actual swap meet. This practice became so popular that it actually evolved into a primary source of income for theater owners. Many added separate swap-and-shop telephone numbers with prerecorded information about swap meet rentals. Concession stand business did quite well as patrons from the swap meet would visit all day long. At many theaters, signs were renovated and adapted to promote the weekly swap meet, which generally took place three times a week. Then, at night, theater operations would continue on as planned.

Another alternative plan, which was also designed to bring in extra income, involved using a theater's lot for a park-and-ride system. The Pacific Theatres branch of ozoners in Los Angeles, California, tried this approach by making an arrangement with the local transit authority, RTD. In this plan, RTD utilized five of Pacific's drive-ins for park-and-ride lots. Commuters paid $2 per month to use the theater as a parking lot and then took the bus to work. It guaranteed Pacific $2,000 a month in extra income. However, the experiment, which was also attempted at the Gemini Twin Drive-In in Dallas, Texas, failed and the project was soon discontinued.

For many ozoners, however, it was still the standard practices of promotion that kept drive-ins going. Personal celebrity appearances were tried and were conducted on a per theater basis. Drive-in chain owner Gordon McLendon happened to be a good friend of John Wayne. When McLendon planned to open the movie *True Grit* at the Gemini Twin in Dallas, Texas, he phoned his good pal and asked him to come out to the theater and make an appearance. Wayne agreed. That night's billing featured a personal appearance not only by the Duke himself, but his co-star Glen Campbell as well. Once the evening started, Wayne shot off his guns from on top of the concession stand and later signed autographs for the moviegoers. The theater was packed, and the show was a huge success.

In another instance, Dallas resident Tony Click recalls the opening night of *Beach Blan-* *ket Bingo* at the Gemini Twin Drive-In. "It was back in the spring of 1965 but, as anyone who's ever been to Dallas knows, it gets hot. Real hot. The stars of the film, Frankie Avalon and Deborah Walley, both appeared that night to promote the new movie. But the thing that stands out in my mind was Deborah Walley's fur coat. It must have been at least 85 degrees and she walked around signing autographs in a full-length mink coat. I thought that was awfully strange, but then again, that's Hollywood." Upon remembering those early drive-in appearances, Avalon recalls, "I always looked forward to going to the drive-in. It was a real treat! In fact, the outdoor movies really helped my movie career!"

Even as theaters tried to stay alive by promoting an occasional family movie, the elements continued to take their toll on old facilities and equipment. Steve Fitch

Although the 1970s proved to be a rather difficult time for ozoners, many large West Coast drive-ins still managed to pull in the dollars by playing first-run pictures. Pacific Theatres

What was once a happy place for families has been reduced to a ghostly time-warp at the edge of town. Here, a lonely Cherokee Indian chief fades in the afternoon sun as he waits for patrons who never do arrive.

Frankie's longtime sidekick and *Beach Blanket Bingo* co-star, Annette Funicello, remembers, "[The drive-in] was a great place to go. It was romantic, exciting, and unusual. It offered kids a great hideaway and had great food—I had a lot of fun at the drive-in the-ater!" Unfortunately for the drive-in industry, not every drive-in owner knew John Wayne or Frankie Avalon and, as a result, celebrity appearances at the ozoner were rather rare.

One final attempt that was made to help sagging business was the introduction of radio sound. An early attempt at such technology was patented in 1951 by R.J. Singleton, a drive-in employee in Hobbs, New Mexico. Unfortunately for Singleton, his method required the installation of a small receiver box in the dashboard. After 30 minutes of rigging, which included drilling holes in the dashboard, the device was attached to the car radio. After this step, the patron could enjoy radio sound. However, the process proved to be too involved and never did catch on outside of Hobbs, New Mexico.

It wasn't until 1970, when Fred J. Schwartz formed a company called Cinema Radio, that radio sound took off. Schwartz had been working on such a system for years, but didn't actually get things moving until he teamed up with engineer William Halstead. Halstead had recently installed a system at Los Angeles International Airport, which used a low-power AM system to broadcast flight

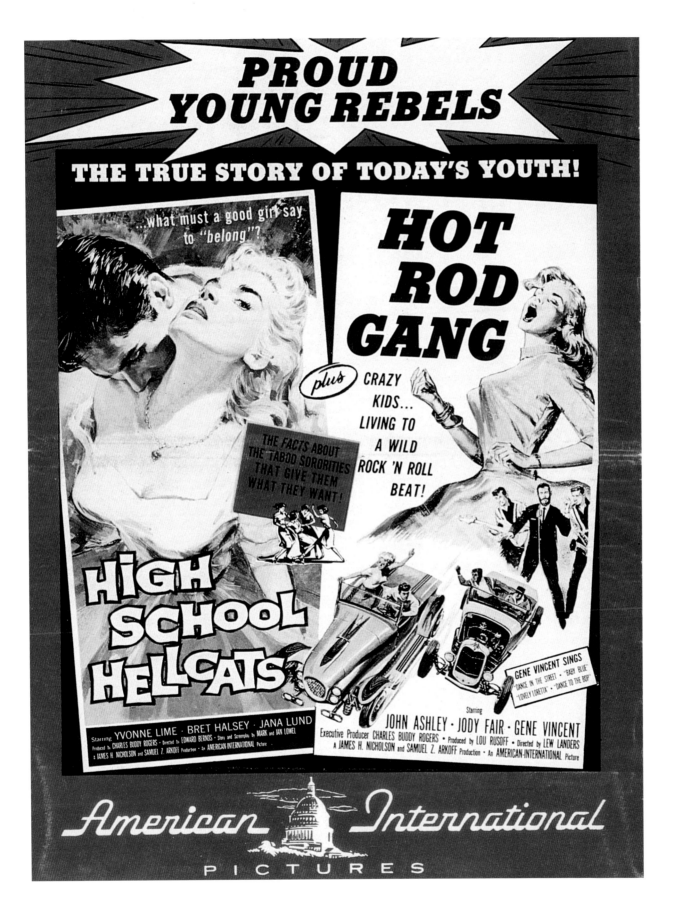

An advertisement for the Halloween Bash at the Porterville Drive-In Theatre. A.J. Roquevert

With bikinis not bringing in the dollars they used to, film producers started to make slightly more risqué films such as High School Hellcats and Hot Rod Gang.

The Skyview Drive-In, a once great outdoor theater, has been left to rot on the Oklahoma prairie.

A once great mural fades in the California sun, but the show goes on at the El Monte Drive-In Theatre.

and terminal information; the system was a perfect prototype for the drive-in project.

The low-power technology consisted of transmitting a specific signal that "leaked" through a special coaxial cable. The cable was then laid throughout the drive-in lot. When a patron parked over the cable and tuned the radio to the proper frequency, the signal could be picked up. Those located outside the theater lot could not tune in the frequency. After 37 years of drive-in sound, the new technology was introduced.

At first, patrons were afraid that running the radio would drain their car's battery. However, Schwartz maintained that a car battery could run a radio for up to ten hours and still use less energy than it would take to start the car just one time. It wasn't long before the system was installed at ozoners across the country. Maintenance was less expensive and sound quality was better. But the dollars

that were sunk into the new system were dollars simply thrown away. Patronage had slipped to an all-time low.

With no healthy income for owners to operate, maintenance became a genuine problem. Many theaters got to the point where they were beyond renovation. Wooden screens were falling apart. If a theater needed to replace a screen tower, it was generally recommended that it be replaced with a more costly steel structure. Weeds and trees sprouted up under the soft soil of back rows. Speaker poles needed to be removed as they were no longer used. Owners couldn't afford the high cost of insurance, so the playgrounds, hamburger grills, and fried food vats all had to go. The panache was gone. The audience had grown up and gone somewhere else.

Movies from the golden years made drive-in fare of the early 1970s look quite dubious. Instead of *The Ten Commandments*,

ozoners were filled with pictures like *The Beach Girls and the Monster*, *High School Hellcats*, and *Billy Jack*. But something strange happened. The scantily clad women of the beach movies no longer attracted crowds. Once again theater owners realized that profits were declining and, in order to survive, they needed income fast. In a desperate move to attract a new audience, operators shifted gears, this time to pornography.

Films like *The Blood Drinker*, *The Shanty Tramp*, *Supervixens*, and *Deep Throat* became the new drive-in rage. Disney simply didn't do the trick anymore. Rather, the only type of film that brought in any money was an X-rated film or soft pornography. And it played huge, in full color, against the night sky. "We kept our kids inside at night and stayed home the first whole summer. We didn't even want to bring a baby sitter up here and expose her to it," explained Sandra Muraski, who lived near a drive-in theater. Her husband Stan went on to say, "I had a very difficult talk with the kids. They were about 10 years old. I had to tell them, 'Adults don't really do stuff like that. Or if they do, they don't let anybody film it.'" But the theaters continued to promote the

only type of movies that would turn a profit. Local churches and community groups tried to close down the theaters. State laws were enacted that made it illegal to exhibit obscene films in places where minors could view the content. The drive-in was now the enemy. "I don't play those R-rated films because I personally want to watch them," explained defensive owner Herb Snow. "I'm in business for economics. I'm showing them to make a dollar. I've been in the theater business eight years and I've sat through one X-rated movie, and I don't care to see another one again."

This shot of the Nevada Drive-In Theatre in Las Vegas, Nevada, was taken in 1973. The theater featured classic art deco lines and spectacular neon lights. Steve Fitch

X-rated films became standard fare at many drive-ins during the mid-1970s. They seemed to be the only type of movie that brought in a crowd. A.J. Roquevert

The last of the "gas guzzlers" line up to watch the movie Sky Tracker as it plays on a Texas screen. Fort Worth *Star-Telegram* Photograph Collection, Special Collections Division, The University of Texas at Arlington Libraries, Arlington, Texas

769-30

A slew of Volkswagen Beetles watch in awe as their hero Herbie in The Love Bug performs a fancy trick under the stars. This publicity still was created by the advertising department of Disney Studios to promote what would become a very popular series of films. The Walt Disney Company

The drive-in had established a new audience and shunned another. It had become a place for "beer movies." If *Climax of Blue Power* was booked one night, operators could not expect kids to show up the next night, even if they booked Disney's *Love Bug*. What parents would feel safe letting their kids run around in such a "weird" place?

Soon drive-ins tried to hide themselves by planting tall, skinny cedar trees or building overlapping wooden fences that would shield motorists from the skin shown on the screen above. It didn't help. Ultimately, the drive-in's image suffered, and pornography and its profits prevailed. It was survival of the fittest.

In 1972 there were approximately 3,342 drive-in theaters in America; this compared to the over 5,000 just 17 years before. Mom-and-pop shops were closing up quickly, and at the same time, cities started growing at a fast rate. Soon, shopping malls were searching for cheap land to construct buildings and parking lots on. The drive-in, usually located at the edge of town and in the direct line of urban expansion, was a prime target. If a corporation such as a Wal-Mart, K-Mart, or Home Depot approached a theater and offered the owner a few bucks for the land, chances

Drive-in owner Gordon McLendon set out to make money by operating drive-in theaters. However, in the end, McLendon made money by selling drive-in theaters. By the time he was ready to build his last three drive-ins, one of which was the Gemini Drive-In, the real estate tycoon realized that drive-in theaters were an excellent way to speculate on land. **Andy Hanson**

A huge, lonely marquee outside Portland, Maine, points the way to a theater that doesn't exist.

were that the money offered was more than the theater would gross in an entire year. Cities continued growing, and by the late 1970s and early 1980s, existing drive-ins were sitting on prime real estate.

"The drive-in was always at the place where the city meets the country." remarks film satirist Joe Bob Briggs. "It was right at the edge of town. The people from the country would drive in to go to it, and the people in the city would drive out to it. In fact, it almost had to be out there because if you had much glare, or if you had many lights, you couldn't see the screen anyway—so it had to be out in cow pasture area. What happened is, as the country grew, that became the most valuable land in the city. The next time the city developed in that direction, there's 14–20

When surrounding neighborhoods could see the movie on the screen tower, many community and church groups lobbied to shut down drive-in theaters. After all, Bellboy and Playgirl *is not for everyone. A.J. Roquevert*

Theaters that once sat along dirt roads on the outskirts of town soon became prime real estate along major highways. Shown here, in the upper left corner, is the Kam Drive-In near Pearl Harbour in Honolulu, Hawaii. On the Hawaiian Islands, property is at a premium. Hawaii State Archives

A rotted-out marquee in Oxford, Mississippi, bakes in the hot sun, fading a little more each day.

Broken-down skeletons of drive-in theaters litter the countryside of America. This place could easily be any small town in the country; it happens to be Lovell, Wyoming.

The wooden frame of a screen tower stands reaching for the sky. The rubble, which stands along historic Route 66 outside of Gallup, New Mexico, is yet another haunting reminder of a bygone era.

A great art deco marquee stands abandoned in East St. Louis, Illinois.

acres, 30 acres, 40 acres all in one piece. You just have to make one sale and there you have a place where you can put an office development or a high-rise or whatever." Gordon McLendon, the one-time owner of several drive-in theaters, admitted that his entire motive for drive-in theater ownership was land speculation. Realizing that it is impossible to tell which way a town might grow, McLendon purchased cheap land and built drive-in theaters on all sides of Dallas, Texas. Years later, when the city surrounded the various theaters, McLendon turned a nice profit by selling the valuable property.

The drive-in was living through desperate times when everything seemed to be pushing it into extinction. With the invention of the VCR, movies could be rented and watched at leisure at home, cable television brought relatively new programming right into the living room, and megaplexes offered up to 30 first-run movies all at one easily accessible location. Even the trusty automobile betrayed its long-time partner. Bucket seats and stick shifts made moviegoing uncomfortable. Drive-ins were meant for real cars—cars that could comfortably sleep eight in the trunk! But Detroit quit making those cars, and as a result, people stopped going to the drive-in.

During the 1980s, ozoners really started to close up fast. Most lots sat vacant for periods of time as business was simply not strong enough to justify staying open. Many owners couldn't even sell the land, as surrounding neighborhoods were too decrepit; no one wanted it. Soon the sad dinosaurs were covered with graffiti and became victims of vandalism. Windows were broken out, projection equipment torn down, and most of the vast lots became covered with weeds and small trees.

The end had finally arrived, or so it seemed.

Blazing Saddles—
A Premiere for Horses

The world premiere of Mel Brooks' 1974 smash hit Blazing Saddles, *which took place at The Pickwick Drive-In Theatre. The event was billed as a "Premier for Horses." No cars were admitted, only horses.* © 1974 Warner Brothers, Inc.

It has gone down in Warner Brothers history as one of the 50 best publicity stunts. In 1974, the Mel Brooks film *Blazing Saddles* was about to open, and like any other film, it needed a good shot of publicity. Fortunately for Warner Brothers, it had a good field publicist on its team in Marty Weiser. Ron Chan, a spokesman for Warner Brothers, remembers that "Marty was regarded as the most talented man who ever worked at the studio." Weiser's idea was brilliant. Instead of booking Mann's Chinese Theater, or some other typical opening night venue, Weiser decided to premiere the film elsewhere, someplace that was directly linked to the integrity of the movie. Weiser booked Burbank's Pickwick Drive-In for the occasion. Realizing that numerous horse stables were located in the nearby Griffith Park area, the event was billed as a "Premiere for Horses." Weiser hung posters in all the stables promoting the one-time event. Only horses were allowed, and each horse could bring one guest. Well, the theater was packed that night, and the stunt worked, making the opening of *Blazing Saddles* one of the most talked-about movie premieres of all time.

And the horseback idea didn't die there. Some drive-in operators in Texas installed rails behind the last row of cars. Horses could be tethered there, and riders could watch the movie from their horse's back. These "gallop-ins" became so popular that owners from northern states even borrowed the concept. Drive-in or gallop-in, both were enjoyable ways to watch a movie under the stars.

Horses and their masters belly up to the "horsepitality bar" during the Blazing Saddles *premiere in Burbank, California. The event has gone down in history as one of the 50 greatest publicity stunts of all time.* © 1974 Warner Brothers, Inc.

Weeds overtake the empty lot of the 49er Drive-In in 1985. Bruce Shinabarger

With its screen still intact and playground equipment waiting, this drive-in stands as a colorful reminder of a simpler time. Steve Fitch

Unfortunately, scenes like this are common throughout the United States. The entrance gates have closed at many ozoners across the nation, including the ones at the Starlite Drive-In in North Reading, Massachusetts. Donald C. Brown, Jr.

Playground equipment sits idle at the old Belknap Drive-In Theatre in Fort Worth, Texas.

CHAPTER 6

THE COMEBACK KID
1985 TO TODAY

In 1958 there were over 5,000 drive-in theaters; today there are fewer than 500 offering 900 screens. Over the years, the outdoor movie scene has greatly changed. In some instances it was for the better, but in most cases it was for the worse. Thankfully, ozoners no longer promote X-rated films or soft-core pornography. The playgrounds and fried foods, however, have been eliminated by insurance costs, leaving theater owners to sell boiled hot dogs, donuts, and boxed candies. It's now a different theater than America grew up with.

In major cities, the old theaters are mostly parking lots or strip malls. The land was simply too valuable to sit idle all day. In rare cases, some metropolitan theaters have survived, due to the support of die-hard owners or nostalgic communities both fighting for the same end.

It's in the small towns across the country that the drive-ins really seem to feel at home. Perhaps it's a lack of local entertainment, or maybe it's still a rite of passage, like learning to ride a bike or taking your date to the Tastee-Freeze. But there's something about small-town people that keeps them coming back to the drive-in. Maybe they just feel at home there.

Good maintenance and presentation keep customers coming back to theaters like the Starlite Drive-In in Milwaukee, Wisconsin. Shown here in the early 1990s, the theater enjoyed first-run films.

The Compton Drive-In in Compton, California, is yet another theater that catered to non-English-speaking moviegoers.

Across the board, city or country, drive-in theaters managed to survive by adapting. And they have more character for it. Each theater has somehow found a way to provide its community with something that it did not previously have. In Reseda, California, the Reseda Drive-In Theatre started courting the large Hispanic population. As opposed to showing movies like *Prisoner of Love*, the Reseda adapted by showing quality Spanish-language films. The same held true for the Compton Drive-In Theatre in south-central Los Angeles. At these theaters, Spanish-language films drew a healthy crowd each week.

The Kar-Vu Drive-In Theatre in Springfield, Colorado, is a recent success story. Here, patrons love the drive-in so much that operator Ruby Ross has to take the popcorn popper out of the local indoor theater (which she operates during the winter) and move it into the drive-in theater. Each season she alternates; indoor theater during the winter months, drive-in in the summer months. The

drive-in is where she does the most business. In fact, during June in Springfield, the Kar-Vu is the only theater in the county.

The Trinity Lutheran Church of Stillwater, Minnesota, still holds its summer worship services every Sunday morning at the Hilltop Drive-In. The sermon is delivered by Pastor Paul Fransen from a small stage set in front of the screen tower. Churchgoers can tune in to the sermon or sing-alongs on the 1100 AM or 87.7 FM broadcast signal. Over the years, the extra income generated by the services has extended the life of the Hilltop as a successful drive-in theater.

Pamela Friend carries on her father's tradition at the Star Drive-In in Montrose, Colorado. The theater recently celebrated its 47th year in operation. When asked about the theater, Friend quipped, "I grew up with this business. I love it!"

Then there are Sam and Carol Kirkland at the Sky-Vue Drive-In Theatre in LaMesa, Texas. The Kirklands had their biggest crowd

3 de marzo

DURO y PAREJO en
La Casita del Pecado

ALFONSO ZAYAS · RAFAEL INCLAN · SASHA MONTENEGRO · ROBERTO "FLACO" GUZMAN · ANDRES GARCIA

A D E M A S

LOS PLOMEROS
...Y LAS FICHERAS

10 de marzo

ALBERTO ROJAS "El Caballo" · PEDRO WEBER "Chatanuga"
MANUEL "Flaco" IBAÑEZ · DIANA FERRETI
CHARLY VALENTINO · JOSE MAGAÑA y GLORIELLA

un MACHO en el SALON de BELLEZA

A D E M A S

SUSANA DOSAMANTES
HUGO STIGLITZ
EL PLACER DE LA VENGANZA
Director: HERNANDO NAME

17 de marzo

VICENTE FERNANDEZ
LALO GONZALEZ "PIPORRO"
EL MACHO

A D E M A S

¡LA FUGA DE CARO!

The advertisement for the Porterville Drive-In lists the variety of films shown in Spanish. A.J. Roquevert

Boris Karloff and the Reseda Drive-In

Boris Karloff, who is best remembered for his portrayal of Doctor Frankenstein's monster, appeared in a rather strange movie that was filmed at a drive-in theater. The picture was called *Targets*. The movie, which was directed by Peter Bogdanovich, centers around an aging horror film star (Orlok, played by Karloff) who has announced his retirement. In the story, as part of a publicity stunt, Orlok makes one final personal appearance at a drive-in theater. However, at the theater, a crazed sniper targets and kills Orlok. Ironically, the film was Karloff's last.

Targets, which did not fare well at the box office, was shot in Los Angeles at the Reseda Drive-In. The theater managed to survive tough times by running quality Spanish-language films.

At the Edgemere Drive-In Theatre outside Worchester, Massachusetts, operators supplement their box-office income by hosting flea markets and swap meets during the day, weekends, and holidays.
Brigham Young University

in over 15 years during the summer of 1995 with over 500 cars attending. And the business just keeps getting better. Sam attributes the success of his theater, in part, to his patented, trademarked food item, The Chihuahua (The Chihuahua even won "Best Food" at the Texas State Fair). The Chihuahua, which is owned by the Sky-Vue Drive-In is, you guessed it, only available at the theater snack bar. In fact, local folks enjoy the taco-like sandwich so much that the Kirklands opened up a separate entrance at the theater. This way patrons can come, purchase

the sandwich, then leave the theater and enjoy the Chihuahua in the comfort of their own home. "We used to close in the wintertime for about two months," recalls Kirkland. "Well, they'd call us at home. Our phone would ring off the wall at home. So we finally decided, we weren't gettin' any peace so we opened it back up. 'Cause they wanted their Chihuahuas... and they missed it."

Bengie's Drive-In Theatre of Baltimore, Maryland, does a swift business and has for nearly 50 years. And they're patriotic, too. If you plan to attend Bengie's, be prepared to

sing the Star Spangled Banner; it's sung every night before the movie starts.

The Edsel Owners Club in Newberg, Oregon, holds a drive-in night each year. The event is a sellout. The same holds true with the Triumph Summer Party held at the Indiana, Pennsylvania, Drive-In Theatre. Here, owners of the vintage British automobiles converge for hot dogs, hamburgers, and a double feature. Various theaters and car clubs across the country frequently work together to host car shows and double features. Not only do these events provide car owners with a nostalgic venue to show off their automobiles, but it gives theaters a great opportunity to boost their annual income.

In 1985, Bruce Shinabarger left his 20-year career with the Tandy Corporation to purchase and operate the 49er Drive-In, which had previously stood abandoned outside Valparaiso, Indiana. Over the next several months he spent weekends at the theater pulling weeds, painting signs, and getting the

Although this photograph depicts a drive-in worship service during the 1970s, the tradition continues today. During the summer, Sunday morning services are held at the Hilltop Drive-In Theatre in Wisconsin's St. Croix Valley. Trinity Lutheran Church, Stillwater, Minnesota

The Kiddieland area equipment, owned and operated by Scott Zimmerman at the Cinderella Drive-In in Englewood, Colorado, is one of the last drive-ins to still have motorized rides. Drive-in owners Jim Goble, Jeff Kohler, and Ken Oborn are proud to maintain this happy tradition at their facility. Jim Goble

Operated by Funtime Drive-In Theatres, Incorporated

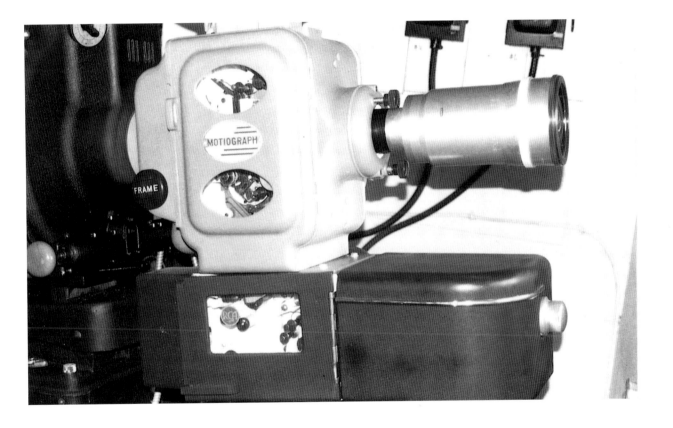

drive-in back into shape. Regarding his dedication, Shinabarger explained, "Sometimes you only have one chance in a lifetime to do what you want to do, and I decided to do it." Shinabarger is certainly a testament to the success of the drive-in theater. When he opened with the film *Twister*, it packed his theater to capacity nearly every single night. The 49er is one of many theaters that has started to book better-quality, first-run features, and it still does a great business today!

Jim Lupima recently bought a run-down theater north of Pittsburgh, Pennsylvania. Like Shinabarger, he too turned the outdoor theater into a booming business. In fact, attendance has been so favorable that he recently purchased a second theater some 60 miles away.

There's even a gentlemen by the name of Carl Harvey, who, with his wife Kathy and dog Pixy, share a rather strange existence. They spend most of their days traveling across the

The Film That Took Drive-Ins by Storm

In the motion picture *Twister*, the 1996 box office smash, a team of Oklahoma meteorologists tracks funnels in a region of the Midwest known as "Tornado Alley." Shot on location at the Beacon Drive-In in Guthrie, Oklahoma, the film features a pivotal scene that takes place in a drive-in theater. In the story, local moviegoers watch *The Shining* as a twister rips apart their small-town drive-in and terrorizes the town. The film, which destroyed the drive-in on screen, did wonders for drive-ins off screen. Drive-ins around the country were sold out as patrons packed the theaters to see the film. Bruce Shinabarger of Valparaiso, Indiana, says, "My theater was sold out for nearly 8 weeks straight." However, what was fantasy on the movie screen in the late 1990s was reality in the early 1970s.

In 1970, in the sleepy town of Miller, South Dakota, moviegoers had settled in for a picture at the Midway Drive-In and were about halfway through the movie when everything went dark. Menacing clouds and lightning were on the horizon. A few cars had decided to leave, but a majority remained. Soon the dust rose from the nearby dirt roads; ketchup, relish, and napkins blew around the concession stand as if there were no gravity. Then the screen went, completely

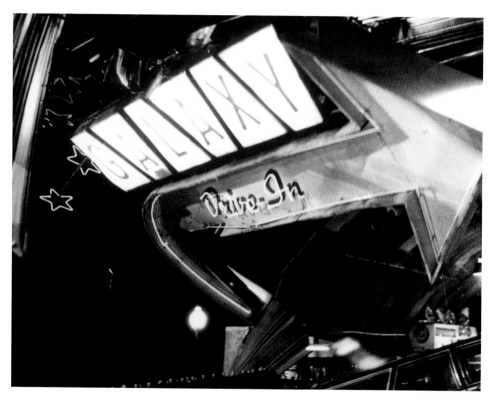

A tornado rips apart the Beacon Drive-In Theatre in Guthrie, Oklahoma, in a scene from Paramount/Universal's Twister. *The film, which was shot on location at the Beacon Drive-In, was credited for bringing incredible business to drive-in theaters across the country.* © 1996 Warner Bros., a division of Time Warner Entertainment Company, L.P. and Universal City Studios, Inc.

blown down by the tremendous winds. A twister had arrived! "It was right in the middle of the movie and the winds just came up out of nowhere," recalls local resident and moviegoer Shirley Aplay. "I knew it was a tornado, and my idea was to get out of the car and lie between the elevated humps in the drive-in lot—to try, somehow, to get to a low-lying area. But my friends wouldn't let me. We just sat there in the car and decided to wait it out. I remember feeling absolutely dumbfounded when I looked up and saw the screen gone. We knew it was bad, but not that bad." Just as quickly as it had come, the storm was gone. The twister had passed leaving the remaining patrons sitting in their cars facing a screen that was no longer there. Oh, and the movie they were watching that night? It was entitled, *On A Clear Day You Can See Forever*.

U.S. looking for drive-in theaters. Carl makes a living as a drive-in screen painter. Based out of Portland, Oregon, Carl and company travel from state to state looking for theaters that need a fresh coat of paint on the white portion of the screen. After finding a customer and bidding for the job (Carl gets over $1,000 per screen), he gets into the gondola of his hydraulic truck and goes to work. When he's finished, it's time to move on to the next town with the next theater. Carl has been painting screen towers for at least 20 years

now and has no plans for retirement.

And where a drive-in is slated to close, drive-in fanatics do their best to keep the memory alive. In the small town of Ocoee, Florida, a suburb of Orlando, the Starlite Drive-In was sold to a developer. Upon hearing this, Ocoee Mayor Scott Vandergriff put together a campaign to purchase the theater and its property. Save Our Startlite (S.O.S.) became the slogan of local nostalgia buffs who formed a non-profit, 501 (C)-3 status organization to back a proposed drive-in

Bengie's Drive-In Theatre is a Baltimore area institution. Patrons are expected to stand and sing "The Star Spangled Banner" before the show. Lawrence R. Loy

145

Jennifer and her staff have brought the 49er Drive-In back to its former glory. The theater sat idle for years before Bruce Shinabarger purchased the grounds in 1985. Bruce Shinabarger

The neon glows brightly at the Family Drive-In Theatre in Stephens City, Virginia. Lawrence R. Loy

In St. Charles, Missouri, the majorette from the Airway Drive-In Theatre was declared a historical landmark before a shopping center was built on the site. The sign now continues to stand on the original property and is complete with moving neon lights. Don Lott

museum inside the theater lot. They held fund raisers and established a Web page to publicize their efforts.

It cannot be ignored that the drive-in theater has become a piece of American nostalgia. The art deco craftsmanship and neon artwork that was used to create many theaters is now on display in museums across the country. The Douglas Auto Theatre sign, which once marked the entrance to the theater of the same name in Kalamazoo, Michigan, is now on display at the Henry Ford Museum in Dearborn, Michigan.

The last of the Mohawks was saved when the Historic Albany Foundation in Albany, New York, stepped in to save the neon sign of the Mohawk Drive-In Movie Theatre. The sign, which represented the vastly changing way of life ushered in by the automobile, now has a new home in the Albany area.

In February of 1995, dedication ceremonies took place at a new Wal-Mart store in Topeka, Kansas, to recognize the preservation of the historic Chief Drive-In Theatre sign. The

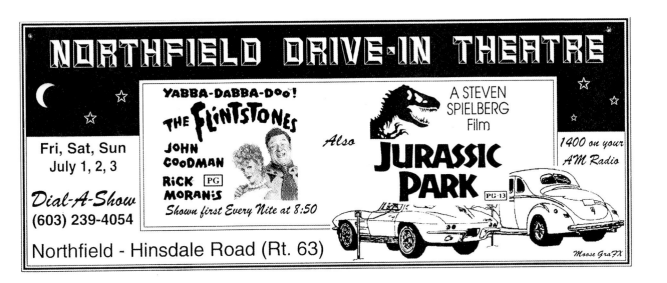

The rocketing spaceship still zooms across the marquee of the Skyview Drive-In in western Illinois.

The Northfield Drive-In Theatre is so large that it is located in two states. Fifteen acres of the theater are located in New Hampshire, and one acre is located in Massachusetts. Interestingly, The Flintstones, *which is promoted in this Northfield Drive-In advertisement, features an opening scene where Fred and Wilma go to the Bedrock Drive-In Theatre. Indeed, the drive-in theater has made many guest appearances in movies and television shows over the years. Programs like "Bewitched," "The Munsters," "Green Acres," and "The Brady Bunch" all chose to film episodes in the drive-in theater.*

Drive-in theater artifacts are now being preserved. The neon-trimmed sign of the Douglas Auto Theatre was moved from the abandoned theater site in Kalamazoo, Michigan, to the Henry Ford Museum in Dearborn, Michigan. The two-scene sign flashes at intervals that make it appear as if the neon car changes from a Model-T to a large, late-model 1950s automobile. Henry Ford Museum and Greenfield Village

Whether they take place during the day or night, classic car shows always draw great crowds to outdoor theaters. Oftentimes, theater owners will host a car club for an evening. At this drive-in, proud owners of restored Plymouths get together for an afternoon car show.
Bruce Shinabarger

The freshly painted playground at this Burlington, Vermont, drive-in awaits its happy summer patrons.

The Drive-In Theatre Fanatic Fan Club is an organization that is dedicated to the memory of the outdoor theater. Each club member proudly carries this swank membership card.

SECRET MEMBERSHIP NUMBER
D.I.T.F.-008-011

colorful porcelain-enamel neon sign, which features the head of an Indian chief in full headdress, dates back to the drive-in's heyday in 1953. Today the sign is still used to promote community events in Topeka.

And when it was announced that a shopping mall was going to occupy the same land where the Airway Drive-In stood, the residents of St. Charles, Missouri, took it upon

themselves to have the art deco sign declared a National Historic Landmark. The contractors had to build around the sign and incorporate it into the architecture of the shopping center. It still stands today as a monument to the Airway Drive-In.

Drive-in fanatics seem to be everywhere. So much so that in October of 1993, Baltimore resident Mark Bialek founded the Drive-In Theatre Fanatics Fan Club. "The organization, which now numbers over 275 members,

Outside Barstow, California, the local drive-in theater awaits sundown and another busy night. Larry Rodkey

Joe Bob Briggs—
The Champion of Drive-In Movies

Famous for his various books and television shows on *TNT* and *The Movie Channel*, Joe Bob Briggs is the self-proclaimed spokesman of drive-in movies. Briggs, who is best known for his work as a film satirist, rates movies based on the "3 Bs;" blood, breasts, and beasts. "*Joe Bob's Drive-In Theatre*" was The Movie Channel's highest-rated show for seven years and was twice nominated for the ACE Award. When reviewing the film *Stone Cold* for the show, Briggs recommended the film based on the film's following qualities:

"[The film is packed with] 62 dead bodies, 12 breasts, 4 fist fights, 4 motor vehicle chases with 4 'crash-and-burns,' 1 pet iguana, face mangling, 'hand-in-the spinning-spokes' torture, a great biker funeral scene, exploding car, exploding judge, heads roll, hands roll, ears roll, everything rolls, kung-fu, pool-stick-fu, tattoo-fu, 4 stars, rated R, check it out and then I'll be back with a couple of erotic thrillers. One of 'em is pretty damned good, the other stars Madonna."

As one might guess, Briggs bases his reviews on the exploitation qualities of each film. When asked about sex and violence in movies he explained, "If you do it in one of these low-budget films, everyone says 'Oh, that movie is full of sex and violence;' but if you do it in an 'A' movie everyone says, 'Oh, that movie is full of romance and adventure." Briggs, who has published six comedy books, written over 250 syndicated radio programs, and appeared on *The Tonight Show* three times, always pops up in the nick of time to defend the beloved drive-in theater.

Drive-in movie critic Joe Bob Briggs is one of today's prime promoters of the American exploitation film. He rates films based upon his system called the "3 Bs": blood, breasts, and beasts. To Joe Bob, the more Bs, the better the film. Mark Hill

At Disney-MGM Studios in Orlando, Florida, The Sci Fi Dine-In Theatre Restaurant offers youngsters a glimpse into the past as patrons eat in their own cars while watching old drive-in movies. Today, the establishment is one of the most popular restaurants at Disney-MGM Studios. © 1996 The Walt Disney Company

Drive-ins have always been known for inexpensive admissions. Even today, ozoners keep admission rates very low. In fact, many still charge on a per-vehicle basis. This theater, located outside Moncton, New Brunswick, Canada, displays its prices in both Canadian and U.S. dollars.

Longtime outdoor theater operator Steve Hull of Hull's Drive-In Theatre. Patrons continue to visit his pristine concession stand nightly for fresh snacks and cold drinks. Debrean Loy

caters to those who want to know more about our beloved drive-in theater. Our chief goal in the Drive-In Theatre Fanatics Fan Club is to familiarize people with the drive-in theater," explains Bialek. "We try to encourage individuals to patronize the theater and use it as an alternative way to view movies. In doing this, we hope that the drive-in can survive our ever-changing culture and continue to thrive into the future." The club's monthly newsletter, which Bialek publishes himself, features articles about old drive-ins, updates about operating theaters, archival advertisements and photographs, and occasional reviews of drive-in-related films, cartoons, stories, and other memories of the outdoor theater. The nationwide fan club is yet another way in which the drive-in refuses to die.

In March of 1995, the Drive-In Theatre Preservation Society was formed for the sole purpose of preserving the Hartford Drive-In Theatre in Bristol, Connecticut. Wal-Mart intended to build a new store on the theater site. However, just one month after the for-

mation of the Theater Preservation Society, the town denied Wal-Mart's application to build on the theater's site. Wal-Mart appealed its case to the Hartford Superior Court, which upheld the decision. The theater still operates today, just as it did when it was built in 1948.

There's even an individual, Joe Bob Briggs, who has launched his entire career by becoming a self-proclaimed public spokesman for the drive-in theater. Briggs, who is actually writer/actor John Bloom, is a fictional character, who loves Texas, America, and the drive-in theater. Over the years, Joe Bob has appeared on national television, written books, and performed one-man shows voicing the plight of the drive-in theater.

Ozoners have felt such a resurgence in some areas that several theater owners have gone so far as to build new drive-ins. Just outside of the sleepy town of Alliance, Nebraska, indoor theater owner Gerald Bullard recently built the Sandhills Drive-In Theatre. Constructed out of telephone poles and plywood, the crude theater stands as a monument to

ozoners of the late-1930s. The screen tower, concession stand, and projection booth were all built by Bullard, who plans to build another theater in South Dakota.

On the Internet, one can find information about Jennifer Sherer, who is gathering information about the construction of new theaters. She plans to build one of her own in the near future. Actually, drive-in Websites are not uncommon on the Internet. Tim Thompson, of Grand Rapids, Michigan, has created a

Web page he calls *The Drive-In Theater*, and believe it or not, over 1,300 individuals visit his site each week. "My main goal is to help bring back some of the fond memories I have of the drive-in," explains Thompson. "A lot of theaters don't partake in the showmanship that was prevalent in the late-1950s, and I simply hope to help people relive that wonderful experience of going to the drive-in." Thompson's Web page features various parts. It has an informational section that

The Spud Drive-In Theatre in Driggs, Idaho, sports a hefty potato as its mascot.

includes a listing of theaters by state, gives information about location, and expounds upon the various promotions offered at the theaters like "family night" or "buck night." There is a historical section which tells about Hollingshead and other important drive-in-related facts. And finally, the Website offers a "virtual concession stand." Here, Web surfers can look at a virtual menu and select from the various food items listed. Upon clicking an icon, a picture of the food item will appear along with a sound effect. Thompson goes on to add, "The theaters here in Michigan are doing a pretty good business and things continue to get better each season. In fact, lots of owners in my area are adding a second, third, or even fourth screen. Just last season our local drive-in in Muskegon, Michigan, extended its season because they had so much trade. Instead of closing in early September like they normally do, they remained open until the end of October. That's just how much business they do!"

Thompson is just one of the many individuals happy to see drive-ins making a comeback. Entertainment giant Disney has even gotten in on the drive-in craze. One of the top-rated restaurants at Disney-MGM Studios in Walt Disney World is the Sci Fi Dine-In Theatre Restaurant. Here, roller-skating waitresses serve up milk shakes and chili fries while patrons dine in replica '57 Chevys. Each automobile faces a giant movie screen that shows schlocky, old teenage films from the glory days of the drive-in. Leave it to the movie studios to recreate the outdoor theater indoors. And companies in show business love to set productions in ozoners. Scenes from something as simple as a music video to something as complex as a feature film can be found taking place in the drive-in theater. Even the opening segment of ABC's Monday Night Football used a drive-in marquee.

Into the Future

After surviving as many successes as it has failures, the drive-in theater stands as one of America's last great icons. It represents youth, freedom, and a national reverence for

At the ozoner in Minden, Massachusetts, a crude yet functional sign turns away customers on a regular basis.

Chuck E. Cheese Pizza Parlors sport this drawing of the happy Chuck E. Cheese characters enjoying a movie under the stars. This specially commissioned piece of art depicts the Chief Drive-In, which was located in Topeka, Kansas. Showbiz Pizza Time, Inc.

The Sky-Vue Drive-In— The Home of the Chihuahua

Just south of LaMesa, Texas, sits the Sky-Vue Drive-In, home of the Chihuahua. Created in 1951, the Chihuahua is the strange taco-like sandwich that seems to bring people back to the drive-in night after night. One hungry patron who held a handful of kitchen towels explained, "... when you eat a Chihuahua, it runs down your elbow kinda like eating watermelon, so we bring our towels so we can clean up." Another added, "It's real messy, but real good!" It seems that everyone in LaMesa loves the sandwich. "The Chihuahua is a real unique sandwich and it's an item that we make right here at the Sky-Vue," explains owner Sam Kirkland. "It consists of two corn tortillas, fried flat, with chili in it, pimento cheese, cabbage, and onions if you want 'em. Then we take one of the corn tortillas and we put our chili on one side. Then, we take the other corn tortilla and we put this special pimento cheese that we make on it. We put the two together and put it in a special Chihuahua sack with a jalepeno pepper. It's the most unusual food item you'd ever think of, but when you put 'em together you don't really taste any one of 'em. It's just got its own little taste... and that's what makes 'em good." Kirkland added that those on dates generally ask to hold the onions.

Sam Kirkland, owner of the Sky-Vue Drive-In Theatre in LeMesa, Texas. La Mesa Press Reporter

SKY-VUE THEATRE & CAFETERIA
DIAL 872-7004   LAMESA, TEXAS

An advertisement for the Chihuahua, Sky-Vue's delicious little sandwich. The trademark food item has been a staple at the Sky-Vue Drive-in since it was invented in 1951. Sam Kirkland

But the Chihuahua isn't the Sky-Vue's only claim to fame. Years ago, the theater's previous owner, Skeet Noret, hired a couple of youngsters to come out and give a musical show from on top of the concession stand—something to entertain patrons while they waited for the movie to start. The result was great music. The people loved the sound, and the show was unforgettable. As the years passed, the wiry little lead singer continued to play venues, each one a little larger than the last. Eventually, he would go on to influence an entire generation of music with a small band that he headlined—Buddy Holly and the Crickets.

Filmack/Mark Bialek

the automobile. Perhaps someday a corporation will build an outdoor theater resort right along the interstate—a perfect tourist trap for those wanting a quick fix of nostalgia. Yuppies will come from miles around so their children can see how grandpa and grandma used to watch movies while sitting in their car. And they'll let young Brian taste a corn dog; maybe they'll even put aside the bottled water and slurp down a soda or two.

And they'll never really know what it was like.

But for every drive-in amusement park that's built, there will exist at least one old woman in some small town who still runs the local drive-in. She'll probably go out every afternoon to chop thistles and chase garter snakes off the property. She'll hang the letters on the marquee herself, changing the sign every week to promote the new movie.

And she'll do it because she loves it.

So, for those who really want to know what it's like to watch a movie, bigger than life, playing against the stars, for those who want to listen as that tinny drive-in sound fights its way out of that squawk box, and for those who want to see the way America used to be, the way America still is in some places, they'll just have to pack up the family wagon and go—to the drive-in theater!

SOURCES FOR FURTHER READING AND VIEWING

Books

(Author). *America Goes to the Movies*. National Association of Theater Owners, North Hollywood, 1993.

Appleton, Victor. *The Motion Picture Chums' Outdoor Exhibition*. Grossett & Dunlap, New York, 1914.

Barell, Barbara. *A Legacy of Light: The History of the Young Sign Company*. Paragon Press, Inc., March, 1995

Cross, Rubin. *The Big Book of B Movies*. St. Martins Press, New York, 1981.

Gebhard, David & Von Breton, Harriette. *L.A. in the Thirties, 1931-1941*. Peregrine Smith, Inc., Salt Lake City, 1975.

Handel, Leo A. *Hollywood Looks at its Audience: A Report of Film Audience Research*. The University of Illinois Press, 1950.

Jackson, Richard H., Shumway, Matthew. *Small Town*. Small Town Institute, Ellensburg, Washington, 1993.

Kindem, Gorham, ed. *The American Movie Industry: The Business of Motion Pictures*. Southern Illinois Press, Carbondale, 1982.

Margolies, John. *The End of the Road*. Penguin Books, New York, 1981.

Mast, Gerald. *A Short History of the Movies*. 3rd. edition. University of Chicago Press, Chicago, 1981.

Matthews, Fred C. *The Design, Construction and Equipment of a Drive-In Theater*. Mitiograph, Inc., Chicago, Illinois.

Miller, Douglas T. and Nowak, Marion. *The Fifties: The Way We Really Were*. Doubelday Press, Garden City, New York, 1977.

Penner, James. *Goliath: The Life of Robert Schuller*. New Hope Publishing Company, Anaheim, California, 1992.

Petersen, George M. *Drive-In Theater: A Manual of Design and Operation*. Associated Publications, Kansas City, Missouri, 1953

International Motion Picture Almanac, (1941-1957). Quigley Publishing Co. Inc., New York, 1957.

Reddick, David Bruce. *Movies Under the Stars: A History of the Drive-In Theater Industry, 1933-1983*. A dissertation. Michigan State University, department of English.

Segrave, Kerry. *The Drive-In Theater: A History from its Inception in 1933*. McFarland & Company, Inc., Publishers, Jefferson, North Carolina and London, 1992.

Sklar, Robert. *Movie-Made America: A Cultural History of American Movies*. Random House Publishing, New York, 1975.

Stanly Robert. *The Celluloid Empire: A History of the American Motion Picture Industry*. Hastings House Publishers, New York, 1978.

Thorp, Margret Farrand. *America at the Movies*. New Haven, Conn., 1939.

Periodicals

1. Advertising Age
2. Boxoffice
3. Business Week
4. Buzz
5. Cinemafantastique
6. Chicago Tribune
7. Christian Science Monitor
8. Current Research in Film
9. Daily Variety
10. Dallas Morning News
11. Drive-In Theatre Fanatics Fan Club
12. Entertainment Weekly
13. Esquire
14. Eyeball Video
15. Film
16. Filmfax
17. Filmmaker
18. Film Daily
19. Film Comment
20. Film Threat
21. Film Quarterly
22. Hollywood Reporter
23. Houston Post Magazine
24. International Motion Picture Almanac
25. Independent Film and Video
26. Literary Digest
27. Los Angeles Examiner
28. Los Angeles Times
29. Midnight Marquee
30. Movie Maker
31. Motion Picture Herald
32. New York Times
33. Newsweek
34. Popular Science
35. Saturday Night
36. Saturday Evening Post
37. Seattle Times
38. Society For Commercial Archeology
39. Texas Monthly
40. Theater Owners Guide
41. Washington Post
42. World of Fandom
43. Variety

Video Tapes

After Sunset: the Life and Times of the Drive-In Theater (45 minutes)

After Sunset follows filmmaker Jon Bokenkamp and three college buddies on a two-week road trip in search of the remnants of a simpler time, the America of lumps in the potatoes, Kool-Aid stands, slow-pitch softball games under the lights, and drive-in movies. Part documentary, part road movie, After Sunset veers onto interesting sidestreets of Americana, but always returns to the main theme. Enlivened by the colorful commentary of drive-in theater owners and notables such as horror film director John Carpenter (*Halloween, The Thing*), film critic and satirist Joe Bob Briggs (*Joe Bob's Drive-In Theatre,* The Movie Channel's highest rated show for seven years), author Michael Wallis (*Route 66: The Mother Road*) and Hollywood movie mogul Samuel Z. Arkoff (*Beach Blanket Bingo*).

Drive-In Blues (28 minutes)

In *Drive-In Blues*, film documentarian Jan Krawitz revisits a lost era of movie-going at cinemas designed for Americans infatuated with the automobile. For 50 years, drive-in theaters asserted their place in American culture as meccas for restless young families and amorous teenagers. These great American icons of post-war prosperity reached their popular apogee in the late 1950s when some 5,000 drive-ins dotted the American landscape. Today, there are fewer than 900. Sprinkled with interviews with drive-in theater owners, *Drive-In Blues* celebrates the heyday of drive-ins and laments their decline.

Internet Site

1. http://www.americandrivein.com

INDEX